1001
FLY-FISHING TIPS

1001
FLY-FISHING TIPS

Expert Advice, Hints, and Shortcuts from the World's Leading Fly Fishers

edited by Jay Nichols
illustrations by Dave Hall

Headwater
Books

This book is dedicated to Lefty Kreh,
who has unselfishly shared with me more tips
than I can count,
and to my daughter, Amelia,
who teaches me new things every day.

CONTENTS

ACKNOWLEDGMENTS

Thanks to the contributors, all expert anglers who not only know their subjects but are generous enough to share with others. This would not be a worthwhile book without them. Special thanks to the staff at *Fly Fisherman* magazine and Stackpole Books for their support, and to artist Dave Hall for the top-notch illustrations.

PART 1

Technique
and Presentation

1

Casting

CAST AWAY

Double over your line to pass it through the guides. After you pull just a short portion of the doubled-over line through the tip-top guide, false-cast the rest of the line and leader out of your rod tip. There's no need to fuss with threading the leader through your guides.

Cracking the Whip

Begin your forward cast too soon and too abruptly, and you might crack the whip. Not only does this sudden unrolling of the line make a loud noise—like a whip—it can cause the outer coating to separate, forming cracks in the front of your fly line. If you see these cracks, don't blame the line company, improve your technique.

PRACTICE RIGHT

Always cast with a practice fly or piece of yarn attached to your leader, and practice casting with different size flies—from White Wulffs to large Deceivers. Different flies require modifications in your casting stroke.

Clip the hook points off with a pair of wire cutters.

Before taking a trip to salt water, practice casting with heavier-weight rods and with large flies, or weighted flies if fishing for bonefish (see "Mousetrap," page 6).

Always wear eye protection. A stray line or leader can damage your eyes, whether there is a fly on your line or not.

QUICK CURE FOR TAILING LOOPS

The quickest cure for a tailing loop—a cast in which the top of the loop ducks below the bottom (on either the backcast or forward cast)—is to point your thumb at the target and raise your elbow slightly after you stop the rod.

STAY IN TOUCH

To improve accuracy, shoot more line than you need to reach your target, and as the fly passes over it, stop the line with your hand. If you shoot line through an O formed by your thumb and pointer finger, you don't have to look down (and away from your target) to regain control of your line and begin retrieving the fly.

CHECK YOUR FLY

Check your fly often to make sure the materials aren't fouled, weeds or debris aren't hanging on the hook, and the point is still sharp (the fly can often hit the ground behind you on your backcast).

Good Delivery

Resist the urge to give your final forward cast something special because it's your last one. Just stop the rod in the direction you want the line to go. Extra effort at the beginning of the stroke can actually reduce or eliminate the potential for acceleration, so start the stroke smoothly and slowly.

ACCURACY CASTING

Cast in an almost-vertical plane for accuracy, but you can cast sidearm on your backcast and come forward straight over your rod tip on your forward cast. This elliptical motion helps avoid tangles—especially with sinking-tip lines.

BACK TO BASICS: LEFTY'S CASTING PRINCIPLES

No matter your style of casting, these principles will help you cast more efficiently, accurately, and farther. Lefty Kreh was the first to codify these principles to help fly casters understand the basics behind their strokes.

Principle 1

You must get the end of the fly line moving before you can make a back or forward cast.

What this means in practice: Ripping line from the water creates a lot of disturbance and spooks fish. Begin the backcast after all the line is off the water and the fly is moving.

Principle 2

Once the line is moving, the only way to load the rod is to move the casting hand at an ever-increasing speed and then bring it to a quick stop.

What this means in practice: This speed-up-and-stop motion is the key to a good fly cast. Focus on accelerating to an abrupt stop.

Principle 3

The line goes in the direction the rod tip speeds up and stops (more precisely, the direction that the rod straightens when the rod hand stops).

What this means in practice: The line continues to go in the direction that you stopped the rod tip, even if you drop the rod tip or move it back and forth to throw slack in the line, such as when making an aerial mend.

Principle 4

The longer the distance the rod travels on the back and forward casting strokes, the easier it is for you to make the cast.

What this means in practice: To make a long cast, extend your arm far back.

QUICK TIPS TO TIGHTEN LOOPS
Stiff Wrist

Any movement with your hand is magnified at the rod tip, so a short movement with your wrist can move the rod tip too much and open your loop. At the first sign of wide loops, focus on keeping a stiff wrist and using only your forearm.

Cast at the Rod Tip

According to Lefty Kreh, this is one of his most effective tips for teaching people to cast tighter loops. As you make your back and forward casts, focus on trying to hit the rod tip with the line.

Squeeze at the Stop

Relax your grip through the stroke, but squeeze the grip to stop the rod quickly at the end.

Improve Haul

Hauling is when you help accelerate the line by smoothly pulling the line with your line hand during the cast. A smooth, well-timed haul can dramatically tighten loops and improve the efficiency of your cast.

Haul Faster, Don't Cast Harder

The harder you cast, the more likely you will destroy your loops by throwing shock waves in the line or twisting your wrist.

Tug a Chain

If you find your haul getting sloppy, slow down and focus on making short, quick hauls—kind of like the motion you'd use to pull a short chain on a basement or closet light. Think of a quick tug rather than a long pull.

CASTING AROUND THE HOUSE

The best time to practice casting is when you are not fishing. Use household objects to practice your stroke.

Rope Casting

Stretch two pieces of rope, garden hose, or bright fly line (use an old line) 4 to 6 feet apart, and stand far enough outside of the ropes so that your rod tip is inside the nearest rope (1 to 2 feet). Try to cast so that your back and forward casts land between the lines. After each back or forward cast, let the line fall to

Rope casting

Hula Loop

Mount a Hula Hoop on a post (or have a friend hold it) and practice casting through it. Begin at 30 feet and move out to 60 feet as you are consistently able to cast a loop through the hoop (not just the fly). Hint: It's easier to cast through the hoop with a sidearm cast than it is with an overhead one. **Improves: Loop size, accuracy.**

the grass, and stop and look where your line went. As soon as you can cast "in bounds" on a 6-feet-wide playing field, reduce the distance to 4. **Improves: Loop size, accuracy.**

Mousetrap

Try to trigger a mouse or rat trap with a weighted fly to improve your accuracy. With this exercise, you'll see that casting sidearm tends to curve weighted flies left or right. Cast vertically over the rod tip for the best accuracy. **Improves: Accuracy, especially with weighted flies.**

Humble Pie

Many casting instructors recommend trying to hit a pie tin at 30 feet, and moving it out a few feet each day to improve both accuracy and distance. Put some water in the pan and your practice fly (a small tuft of Glo Bug yarn) won't bounce out as easily. **Improves: Accuracy, distance.**

Toss a Rock

To visualize the proper hand motion for a sidearm backcast, pick up a rock, block, baseball, set of keys, or wallet and toss it behind you toward a target. **Improves: Casting stroke and stop.**

Paintbrush

Dip a 4-inch paintbrush in water to practice your speed-up-and-stop. If you make a long sweep, the water (line) goes all over the place (good thing you are not using paint); make an accelerated speed-up-and-stop, and the paint (line) travels in one direction. **Improves: Stroke and stop.**

Hammer a Nail

Stopping your rod at the end of a back or forward cast is similar to the sudden stop of a hammer hitting a nail—and the hand position is also nearly identical. **Improves: Stroke and stop.**

Swing a Bat

Envision hitting a ball with a bat. As you swing, your grip is relaxed; at the moment of contact, you squeeze. It's the same with the casting stroke—relaxed through the stroke, squeezing when you stop on the forward and backcasts. **Improves: Grip.**

Play Ball

Casting Principle 4 (page 4) states that the longer you move your rod through the stroke, the easier it is to make a long cast. It's the same with throwing a baseball or softball. To make a short throw, you move your arm through a small distance; to make a long throw, you extend your arm and move it through a greater distance. **Improves: Stroke and stop.**

Flying Fruit

Fling a potato or apple off a stick. Pierce a small apple or potato with the end of a stick. Practice throwing the apple at targets in front of and behind you. **Improves: Speed up and stop, stroke.**

Snap a Towel

Put your high-school locker-room skills to good use and snap a towel at a target behind you. **Improves: Speed up and stop.**

Cast on the Shelf

Since many people tend to raise their elbows too high when they cast, especially on the backcast, Lefty Kreh suggests keeping your arm on a shelf through the stroke. While a banister or countertop will help you train your stroke, even better is to build a ramp with a slight incline. The proper motion of a good backcast is a slight upward climb along a shelf. **Improves: Loop control, backcast.**

Fly on the Wall

Practice keeping the rod tip in line and your hand straight through the casting stroke by practicing your casting motions while standing next to a wall. The wall prevents you from twisting your hand outward, which is a prime culprit of wide loops. **Improves: Loop control.**

GRASS LEADER

Practicing Spey casts on grass is typically not very effective because you need the water's grip on the fly line to help load the rod. To simulate this grip, fashion a special leader that catches the grass enough to help load the rod. It's not perfect, but it is better than nothing.

Some recommend building a grass leader with 8 to 14 feet of 20-pound Maxima tied in 7- to 10-inch sections with blood or surgeon's knots. Leave tags on and trim to suit ($\frac{1}{4}$ to $\frac{3}{4}$ inch long). Use longer tags for casting on the snow.

Others make leaders 4 to 6 feet long from 3 or 4 sections of 30-pound-test Maxima or other stiff monofilament. Start with long tags and modify as needed to get the desired results. Leader length, length of the tags, and height of grass affect the "load."

Improve Your Double Haul

Lefty Kreh

After learning the proper hauling motions, most casters still need to improve their timing and efficiency.

Learn or refine your double haul by casting on the grass, and taking the time to stop in between your back and forward casts to think about what you are doing.

Cast with only a few fingers (thumb, pointer, and middle) holding the rod grip to force you to increase line speed through the haul only.

Use only the top half of a fly rod to learn to haul more efficiently. String your line through the guides of the half rod. Since you have no handle, hold the rod with your pointer finger stretched along the blank.

Mirror the haul with the speed-up-and-stop of your rod. When you stop the rod, stop the haul. The longer you move the rod through the stroke, the longer your haul should be.

GOING THE DISTANCE

Casts over 60 feet are rarely necessary in fresh water, but being able to cast 90 means that you have mastered line speed and loop control. Plus, you may need that 90-foot cast to cast 60 feet in a wind.

Stretch your line before casting. (See "Get the Kinks Out," page 105.) Coils in your line rob your cast of distance, affect accuracy, and make it harder to set the hook on a fish.

Use a stripping basket or Line Tamer to help prevent tangles and cast farther.

Learn to shoot line on the backcast. This also helps you cast more line quickly without false-casting. On your final backcast before your delivery stroke, shoot several feet of line to help load your rod.

Extend your rod far back. A fly rod is a flexible lever. The longer your stroke, the more efficient your cast.

Make an O with the thumb and pointer finger of your line hand to shoot line through. Your fingers act like an extra shooting guide and eliminate many tangles (see "Taming Tangles," page 12.)

Clean and lubricate your line. Most modern fly lines are self-lubricating, but they need to be regularly cleaned of grit and grime. Mild dish soap and a face cloth do the job at home, but in the field, single-use line-cleaning pads are more convenient.

Mirror right hand with left. Refine the timing of your double haul so that you make a longer haul that mirrors the long rod motion and you stop the haul when you stop the rod.

Focus on Footwork

Different distance casters have different stances. Most advocate casting with the right foot back (right-handed casters) because that gives you the widest range of motion with your body. Some advocate putting the right foot forward because that stance allows them to stop faster on the forward cast. All adopt a relatively wide, shoulder-length stance for balance and range of movement. Pay attention to how your stance helps or hinders your cast.

Stretch your fly line

Casting Weight

Bob Clouser

Modify your stroke when casting weight—this includes weighted lines, weighted flies, and split shot.

Roll cast a sinking line to the surface so it is straight before beginning your backcast.

Prevent tangles by casting around in a half circle. Make a low, slow backcast sideways and come forward with a vertical cast aimed above eye level. Think of pulling the line around the inside of a horseshoe turned on its side. This cast is sometimes called a Belgian or elliptical cast.

Open your loop by speeding up and stopping your stroke over a longer distance. Forget those tight, dry-fly loops. Slow down your casting stroke. Don't false-cast at all if possible.

Water haul sinking lines; don't false-cast them. For the single water haul, roll cast the sinking line to the surface. Water tension loads the rod

Cast around in an oval

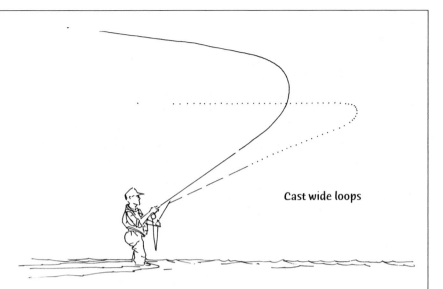

Cast wide loops

and sets up a good backcast. Make your backcast, shooting line if you want, and present the fly on your forward cast.

Double water haul. Follow the steps for a single, but on your backcast, let the line land straight on the water behind you. Begin your forward cast before it sinks.

Watch your overhang. Overhang, the amount of running line outside of your tip guide, is critical when casting shooting heads. Too much overhang causes shock waves in your line and poor casts. Too little overhang robs you of distance. Start with only the shooting head outside of your rod tip and keep the thin running line inside the line guides. Gradually use more overhang until you determine the proper amount for best loop shape and distance.

See tips for preventing tangles in running line, page 12—you'll need them.

Shoot line on the backcast for extra distance before your final delivery cast.

TAMING TANGLES

Line Tamer

Control your line with a stripping basket or Line Tamer (see "Make Your Own Stripping Basket," page 142), also called a vertical line management device (VLMD), when wading in deep water or fishing from a boat.

Hat Trick

Tuck a baseball hat (hat brim first) into your wading belt, and strip line into its crown if you don't have a stripping basket handy.

Go Barefoot

Shoelaces and straps catch fly lines. Go barefoot or wear socks when fishing from the casting platform of a boat (if weather allows).

Keep It Wet

A bit of water in your stripping basket or VLMD keeps the line slick and prevents tangles.

Clear the Boat

Eliminate objects that can tangle your line—before you start fishing.

Cover Up

Cover boat cleats with duct tape. Cover engines, gas tanks, and other objects in or near the transom with a small net.

Watch the Prop

If fishing out of a boat with an engine, watch out for the prop. Make sure that you reel in line or stow it in a stripping bucket before the captain moves the boat.

Stretch Your Line

The tight coils produced by your reel are the most common source of tangles. On shore, wrap your line around a fence post or tree; in a boat, stretch the running line by hand one arm-length at a time.

Tilt the Reel

When shooting line, some anglers advocate tilting the reel handle away from the line to prevent it from catching and to reduce friction through the guides.

Extra Stripping Guide

Shoot line through an O formed by your thumb and your middle or pointer fingers—don't let go of it.

BEATING THE BREEZE

Sometimes the best dry-fly fishing occurs when a wind funnels bugs along a shore or drift line and the chop on the water masks your approach. In the salt or on trout streams in the West, wind is a fact of life.

Wind in Your Face

Shorten your leader. Wind buffets long leaders and sends them astray, making accurate casts impossible.

Change flies. Bulky, bushy flies are difficult to cast in the wind. Try using compact, weighted flies such as Clouser Minnows, beadhead nymphs, and conehead streamers.

Cast farther. With a stiff wind blowing in your face, you may have to cast 60 feet of line to get 40. It's hard to be accurate under these conditions.

Get closer. While wind may blow your line around, the chop on the

Switch to a Sinker

Hang up the floating line and use an intermediate or sinking shooting head, if it's practical. Because they are heavier and thinner, these lines punch through the wind better than floating lines.

water allows you to get closer to your target.

Cast tight loops. Wide loops are not as aerodynamic or efficient as tight loops (see "Quick Tips to Tighten Loops," page 4).

Aim at the water, not above the water. The higher you aim the forward cast, the more the wind can blow it around. A gentle presentation is less important when the wind is strong and the water choppy. Aim your tight loops toward the water, dropping the rod tip after the stop so that the line that isn't unrolling lies against the water where it can't be blown around.

Cast sidearm. Not only can you throw tighter loops, but your line is closer to the water and less likely to be blown around by the wind.

Triple haul. After your second haul, add yet another short, fast haul to help turn over the fly and leader.

Better Backcasts

Ed Jaworowski

Fly fishers don't pay enough attention to their backcasts. Without a good backcast, you can't have a good forward cast.

Look at your backcast. You can't fix it unless you know it's broken.

Film your casting (set up a camera on a tripod) and analyze your mistakes later.

Before you cast, get as much slack out of the line as possible and begin with your rod tip low to the water for long casts.

Make your initial motion slowly, and when the line is taut to the tip continue accelerating to a quick stop.

Aim your backcast opposite your target.

A firm wrist prevents wide loops.

Wind on Your Casting Arm

This annoying, potentially dangerous wind can blow the fly into you.

Cross the river—if you can.

Cast cross arm. Bring your rod hand up to your left ear (if you are a right-handed caster) to keep the line on the far side of you.

Turn around and present the fly on your backcast. Saltwater anglers, who have to constantly deal with wind, have perfected this cast that also works well for freshwater fishing, especially when using streamers and other wet flies. Simply turn away from your target (180 degrees is best) and let it fly on your backcast.

Begin your forward cast while the backcast is still unrolling, not after it has straightened completely. This helps you begin your forward cast slowly and accelerate to a stop. The rod will load instantly, you will have a longer effective stroke requiring less force, and you will finish with the rod tip and line going forward, rather than down.

The longer your cast, the farther you need to move the rod. The key to making longer casts without casting harder is to start with the rod pointing back farther, even to straight back, for the longest casts. This will load the rod deeper.

Prevent tailing loops on your backcast by stopping the tip while it is traveling in a straight path and accelerating so that the top of the loop stays on top.

Refine your double haul to efficiently generate the high line speed required to turn over your backcast on longer casts.

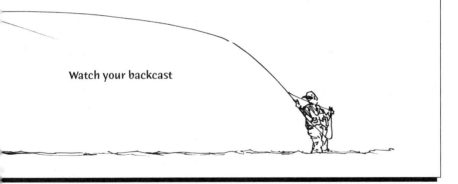

Watch your backcast

Wind at Your Back

This wind can make you look like a casting superhero—if you have a good backcast.

Perfect your backcast. Because you are driving your backcast right into the wind, your technique needs to be very good. Learn to cast a tight loop with high line speed, and perfect your haul.

Fly a kite. After you cast a low tight loop on your backcast, come forward with a vertical cast aimed higher than eye level. Your backcast can be short; shoot line on your forward cast for distance. The wind will take your line out like a kite.

Spey-Casting Basics

Simon Gawesworth

Spey casts are change-of-direction casts with two- or single-handed rods and, though traditionally used for salmon and steelhead fishing, are opening up new opportunities for trout and saltwater species.

Get a grip. Spread your hands far apart for the most comfortable, powerful grip. To fit your grip, hold the rod loosely in your right hand at arm's length. (Left-handed casters, use your left hand.) Slide the rod through your right hand until the butt grip nestles comfortably under your right armpit. Where your right hand is holding the rod is the best place to grip it for casting efficiency with longer belly lines. With short-head lines like Skagit lines, slide your upper grip closer to the reel. Rest your lower hand at the lower end of the butt grip.

Find the balance point. Find the rod's point of balance with the reel to help you cast with the least amount of effort. Where the rod balances on the finger is where the upper hand should grip the rod. The farther away from the balance point you hold the rod, the more work you have to do and the more you strain your muscles. Adjust the weight of the reel to ensure the balance point agrees with the grip above.

Listen for the Slurp

The more line touching the water at the start of the forward cast (the stick), the more effort you'll need to break it out of the surface film with the forward stroke. To tell if you have too much stick on the water, listen for the telltale slurp of line as you begin your forward cast. The louder the slurp, the more stick there is. Several culprits contribute to slurp, but begin your forward cast sooner next time and see if that helps.

Match the reel to the rod. For reels, the usual guideline is three sizes up from the Spey line. If you have a #8 Spey line, get a #11 reel, though it does depend a lot on the head length of the Spey line. A properly balanced rod and reel should balance somewhere near the top of the grip. Too far forward and the reel is too light; too far back and the reel is too heavy.

Tape the Ferrules

Because Spey casting involves a lot of direction changes that can twist the rod, check your ferrules often to make sure they are seated properly. Use electrical insulating tape to secure the rod sections.

Generally, use both your top and bottom hands equally. Most people overpower the cast with their top hand and don't use their bottom hand enough. The bottom hand should finish the cast close to or touching your chest. With long-belly lines 75 percent of the power should come from the upper hand. With short-head lines, 75 percent of the power should come from the lower hand.

The larger the belly/D-loop in your fly line, the less effort you need on the forward cast. The most efficient belly/D-loop is 180 degrees from where you want the forward cast to go.

Big figure-eights and loops look pretty, but they do little to improve distance or efficiency. A downward-moving rod tip cannot move the line forward, or back, an inch. The only direction that really affects how far a line will travel is horizontal.

Two-handed rods are long and even the slightest movements with your rod hands are magnified at the tip. Even small movements can cause big loops, so keep your stroke compact and make sure the rod tip travels in a straight line.

Tandem Flies

Charles Meck

Tandem flies, also called multiple-fly rigs, are a versatile way to cover different depths in the water column, match several types of food at the same time, or give fish the option of different colors, shapes, and sizes of flies to determine which one they prefer. But casting two or three flies at once requires some adjustments. For more information on fishing multiple flies, read Fishing Tandem Flies, *Headwater Books, 2007.*

Be prepared for the worst. Though you can minimize them, tangles are a fact of life with tandem-fly rigs. Carry extra leader and tippet to rebuild rigs, build the mental stamina to patiently pick out a wind knot, and learn to recognize the times when you must cut the flies off and start over.

Cast open loops. Forget the tight loops that everyone talks about—they only make matters worse. Open up your loop by widening your stroke and pointing your thumb at the target when you stop the rod.

Cast around in a circle. Flies collide when you cast in a straight back-and-forth motion. Instead, begin your backcast at an angle to the side and bring your forward cast over your right shoulder (if you are a right-handed caster).

Stiffen up. Fluorocarbon tippets, which are generally stiffer than monofilament tippets, tend to tangle less.

Keep it short. Until you learn how to cast multiple flies with minimal tangles, keep the distance between the flies short. Often, 12 to 18 inches is adequate.

Taper Down

Use progressively lighter tippet to connect each fly. If you are fishing a dry-and-dropper rig, connect the dry fly with 5X and the nymph with 6X. This makes it easier to cast and prevents you from breaking off all the flies should you snag your bottom fly.

OVERLINING AND UNDERLINING RODS

Line-weight designations are only manufacturers' recommendations for each rod (see "AFTMA Line Chart," page 107). Most rods can handle several line weights, depending on the caster's skill and the distance cast. Sometimes it pays to overline or underline your rod depending on circumstances.

Overline To

Turn over large flies. More fly-line mass helps turn over larger flies, especially if you are fishing a fast-action rod that can handle one to two line weights higher than what it is rated for. If you like fishing for bass on a 5-weight, but you will be casting poppers and Clouser Deep Minnows, try uplining to a 6-weight line.

Cast in Tight Quarters

Make short casts on small streams. Casts are often less than the 30 feet for which the rod is rated. Upline one size to help you load your rod in short.

Feel the load. Loading a rod completely (but not overloading it) helps you cast more efficiently, yet most casters never load the rod well. To feel a deeply loaded rod, try casting a line weight one size heavier than what is rated for your rod.

Convert your fast-action rod to a slower-action one. Many of today's fast-action rods are too stiff for some people's preferences. You can get a slightly slower action if you overline the rod.

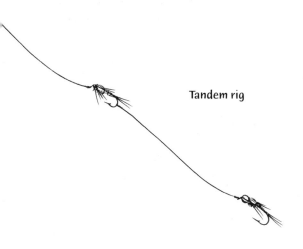

Tandem rig

Underline To

Make more delicate presentations. Line weight, size of fly, and length of leader effect presentation more than rod weight.

Carry more line. Sometimes you need to pick up a long line and cast it back out quickly, such as when fishing to specific targets from a drifting boat.

Cast for distance. If you typically carry and cast more than 35 to 40 feet of line, you might find it easier to underline your rod. For every 10 to 15 feet added to the 30 in the air, you add another line weight to the load—a 5-weight line becomes the equivalent of a 6-weight when 40 feet of line is aerialized, a 7-weight with 60 to 65 feet in the air, and so on.

Beat the breeze. Smaller-diameter line is less air-resistant than large-diameter line; however, if you try to trick the wind with a lighter line weight, keep in mind that you have to aerialize more of it to load the rod.

2

Wading

PATH OF LEAST RESISTANCE

It is difficult to wade directly across a river and even more fatiguing to wade up and across. The easiest, safest path is usually at a slight downstream angle. If you angle downstream, you will tire less quickly and tend to fall less since you are not fighting the current with each step.

CAUTION IN THE COLD

In cold weather, be more conservative with your wading because the cold water tires you out more quickly.

PICK A GOOD STAFF

The collapsible ones are good for mild currents, but as advertised, they can collapse. Lefty Kreh likes a wooden staff that floats behind him when not in use; Dick Galland recommends using an old ski pole.

If you normally don't use a wading staff, but find yourself in a tough wading situation, even a stout tree limb is better than nothing.

THIRD LEG

Your wading staff should act as a third leg. Plant one foot and the wading staff firmly before advancing the other foot. Make sure both feet are stable before you plant your wading staff.

Go with the Flow

If you fall in, don't panic and fight the current. You will not sink if your waders fill with water. Point your feet downstream with your head up and your arms outstretched. Deflect rocks with your legs and arms to avoid hitting your head. The current will eventually take you close to shore or to shallow water.

Wading Basics

Dick Galland

Smart wading begins with common sense.

Don't wade unnecessarily. Wading is not appropriate in all waters. The fish are much less likely to be alerted to your presence if you stay out of the water. The pressure wave you create as you wade spooks fish, especially in slower pools.

Wade with respect for the fish and other anglers. Every step you take disturbs the aquatic ecosystem. Avoid weedbeds; they are the condos for the bugs. Avoid wading through spawning redds. Be mindful of how your wading affects nearby anglers. Your wading can stir up the bottom and impact the fishing downstream.

Take appropriate safety precautions. A wader belt is as important as a seatbelt. Buckle up every time you go out and cinch it high on your chest in deeper water to trap as much air as possible and prevent water from coming in. Wear footwear that increases traction. Use a wading staff. In rocky freestone water, with varying depths and current velocity, the angler with a staff will outfish the wader without a staff every time and will swim less.

Lean into the current. Always plant your staff upstream of your body, leaning into the current. Should you begin to lose your balance, the current will push you upright rather than downstream.

Keep your body sideways to the current. Facing directly upstream or down exposes you to the full force of the water and makes it difficult to maintain your balance.

Shuffle. Move your feet along the bottom as though you are blind. Use your staff to check ahead for changes of depth or obstacles. Keep a wide stance. Feel along with each foot and find a secure spot before you commit your weight to it.

Know your limits. When the water reaches your knees, wading becomes more difficult. If you have limited wading skills, don't go in above your knees in fast water. The deeper the water, the more buoyant you become and the less traction you have. There is a point of no return when you are at the mercy of the current, even if your feet are still touching the bottom. Learn to anticipate that point and to stop before you reach it.

Conserve energy. Cross on a slight downstream angle wherever possible. When fishing upstream, walk the bank or in the slow currents along the side and use the eddies created by rocks in the current to ease your passage. Move from eddy to eddy in a bouldery river. Those little pockets of still water below rocks give you a moment's rest. Go around boulders, rather than up and over them. The less climbing the better.

Plan your route. Look downstream for obstacles and hazards you will have to deal with if you lose your footing. If there is particularly hazardous water below, consider crossing or wading elsewhere. Think about what you'll do if you're swept away. Look for the places where you might get into an eddy. Look for obstacles that might trap or injure you.

Team Up

In big water, wade with a buddy. Have the strongest wader take the upstream side. Tuck your rod into your waders or vest. Lock arms, or, better yet, grab the collars of one another's vests with your inside hands and plant your staves with your outside hands. Talk to one another as you progress across the river.

continued on page 24

Wading Basics continued

Don't die for your tackle. If you are swept off your feet, you might be able to tuck your rod butt down into the front of your waders or throw it to shore, but don't risk your life for a rod. Your recovery will be considerably easier with both hands free.

Practice swimming with your waders on in a river or swimming pool. This helps to mentally prepare you in case you fall in. Have a friend nearby for safety.

Learn to self-rescue. If you fall in fast water, turn on your back and imagine that you're a drift boat: Your feet become the bow, your head the stern, and your arms the oars. Scan the water downstream, pointing your feet at the obstacles you want to avoid and backstroke into the current with your arms. Position your body at 45 degrees into the current and stroke toward the shore. Backstroking will move you away from any obstacle downstream and toward the shore in a relatively straight line. Wait until you are in slow water before you try to stand. Get out of the cold water as fast as possible.

Remember the acronym WADER. Wear your wader belt. **A**ssess the difficulty and anticipate the problems. **D**evelop a plan. **E**xecute that plan. **R**etreat if necessary.

PLAN FOR THE WORST

Carry a change of clothes and socks in a waterproof bag in case you fall in. You can leave them in the truck if you are fishing nearby, but take it with you if going in a boat. Keep cell phones, camera, wallet, and any other valuables or electronics in a dry bag. A Ziploc baggie provides inexpensive insurance against rain or a quick spill.

Inflatable PFDs (personal floatation devices) built into fanny packs or fishing vests are wise investments for potentially dangerous wading environments such as fast freestone rivers or jetties in salt water.

Carry a book of matches in a watertight container. If you get stranded or fall in the water, you can make a fire to keep yourself warm. Always carry a whistle with you when you're fishing alone— even when you're on the bank.

WADING THE SURF

Several anglers die each year wading the ocean's currents. Fishing at night compounds the danger.

Move frequently. The undertow can pull the sand out from under you.

Swim perpendicular to rip currents if you get caught in one. Swim to shore only after you are free of the rip current—don't try to swim directly against it.

Tails, You Win

The shallowest part of a river is often at the tail of a pool, so look for these areas when crossing—especially crossing unfamiliar water—even if it means walking a ways to find one. Also, evaluate the stream bottom. Sand and small rocks indicate slower currents and are easier to wade than bowling ball–size rocks covered with algae.

Tail of pool

Know the Tides

A rising tide may strand you on a sand bar that you were able to wade out to in lower water, or wash you from a jetty that was dry at low tide.

Stripping baskets can be dangerous in the surf. Drill extra holes in the bottom so the water drains quickly or use one with a mesh or net bottom. Better, learn to manage your line without a basket if you wade in rough surf.

Aluminum cleats are essential footgear when scrambling over rocks.

Wear an inflatable personal floatation device (PFD) in the surf and when fishing jetties. Several manufacturers make Coast Guard–approved PFDs that fit in suspenders or a fanny pack.

Drill drain holes in your basket

TAILWATERS

On some tailwaters, water levels can change quickly and without much warning. On many tailwaters, such as the White River in Arkansas, rising water often creates good fishing conditions, so anglers are tempted to continue to fish even when it's not safe to wade—don't.

Bullhorns, lights, or both often signal when the water is going to start rising. Pay attention to these signs.

In hot weather, a fog bank or cold blast of air coming downriver often signals rising water.

Monitor a log, rock, or section of streambank to detect whether water is rising if you are downstream or out of earshot of the dam. Sometimes you will be so busy fishing that you may not notice until it's too late.

Plan an escape route before you start fishing. Identify shallow bars where you can cross.

Watch the signs. Debris, foam, or increased bird activity may signal rising water.

WET WADING

Wading wet in the summer simplifies your gear and cools you off. When hiking and fishing, you sometimes have no choice.

Unwadered legs are more sensitive to temperature change. If the water feels like bathwater, don't fish for trout.

Wear nylon (or other quick-drying material) shorts or pants when wading wet to prevent sunburn and scratches from trees and shrubs. Cotton takes longer to dry. Bring along a change of clothes if you have a long car ride home.

Wading sandals are great for sandy bottoms, but wading boots are best where sharp rocks can cut your feet.

Wading boots are sized for waders. Buy a pair of neoprene socks for wet wading or take up the extra space in your boot with two pairs of socks.

Bring along a pair of Tevas or other water sandals for stream crossings so you don't get your hiking boots and socks wet, or wear synthetic socks that are still functional even when wet.

Find Spring Holes

Wet wading is a great way to find spring holes, which attract fish in summer and winter.

In a pinch, trash bags over your feet (and under the hiking boot) will keep your socks dry if you have to cross a stream in the backcountry.

3

Finding and Spotting Fish

LOOK AROUND

Nearby banks provide clues to the bottom of the river or lake. If you see big rocks and stones on the bank, the stream bottom nearby is probably similar and good holding water for fish. Move on if the banks are silty. Steep banks often mean deep water; gradually sloping banks often mean shallow water that deepens gradually.

FOCUS ON THE FOAM

Foam lines moving downstream signal current lanes that carry food to fish and are always a good place to start fishing.

BE FIRST TO THE FISH

This doesn't mean that you should rush to fish a particularly good pool before your buddy gets his rod rigged up, but if you are fishing behind another angler, especially a careless one, you may never see a fish—they will all have spooked.

Focus on the foam

FIND SOLITUDE

Fish during the week, fish early and fish late, and walk a lot to find the best fishing.

FISH FROM THE OTHER SIDE

Cross to the side of the river opposite the road or access trail. Most anglers don't walk far from their cars, and most don't bother crossing to the other side of the river.

LOOK FOR THEM

Instead of fishing blind, walk along the banks until you spot fish. You'll spend more time walking and looking instead of casting, but this is how the guys who consistently catch big fish do it.

SCOUT IT OUT

Low water may not be the best time for catching, but it's the perfect time to look for hidden holes, lies, and bars in the middle of the river. In the summer, wet wade to find cooler water where springs might come in—fish migrate there in summer and winter.

Change Is Good

Changes in current speed, depth, water temperature, and stream bottom all provide clues to a fish's location. If you are new to a particular stretch of water, look for change, and start fishing there. This holds true in fresh and salt water. Color changes are subtle but especially important. A change from light green to dark green in a river often indicates a depression and is likely to hold fish. Dark spots on a saltwater flat indicate a grassy bottom.

Finding Fish in Big Water

Scott Sanchez

Large rivers may be intimidating at first glance, but successful anglers divide and conquer.

Break it down. Large rivers have the same structure—riffles, inside corners, runs, pools—as small streams, they are just bigger.

Big fish can swim in shallow water. Just because the river is large doesn't mean that you have to fish far out.

Side channels fish just like small streams. Since drifts boats rarely venture to these areas, they are not as heavily fished as the main river.

Riffle drop-offs and seams indicate prime habitat. Shallow riffles are the grocery stores of aquatic insects, and deep drop-offs provide havens from predators. Look for the signature tan to green color. Large river seams are great places to fish. The conflicting currents make a void for the trout to swim in and funnel food their way.

The correct speed for a fishing bank varies with water levels. You need enough current to keep the trout in place, but not so much they can't swim in it.

Boats make it easier to fish big water where wading is limited and can take you to less-pressured wade fishing.

Wading water. Braided sections of large rivers offer some of the best fishing. Think of them as multiple streams. They are great habitat, but also easier to wade. Make sure it is legal to wade, and use caution.

Use gear big enough to get the job done. Big rivers are often windy. Larger (6- to 7-weight) rods and stout tippets help you make longer casts with larger flies that imitate the insects (stoneflies and terrestrials) on many Western waters. Heavier tippet gives you the ability to lean on fish that get out in the current and have room to run.

Use small enough gear. Many Western tailwaters have prolific hatches of small insects. A lighter rod long enough to mend (8½- to 9-foot, 3- or 4-weight) is ideal for fishing small fly hatches, and a soft rod makes it harder to break light tippets.

Sight-Fishing Secrets

Landon Mayer

The more fish you see, the more you catch.

Look, then fish. Before you start casting, look for targets. Casting blind may spook wary fish.

Get high. Elevation helps you see into the water. If you can, climb a high bank, but keep a low profile while you scout the stream.

Double team. Working with a partner is fun and effective. One person spots the fish from on high and calls out directions to the angler in the stream. Plan ahead how you will mark the fish—"two feet upstream of the big boulder" (see "Telling Time," page 34). Switch after each fish.

Wear polarized glasses. Good glasses matter and can mean the difference between success and failure. Polarized glasses remove glare from the water's surface and provide a better view of the river bottom. They come in different tints to help you see better under a wide range of conditions.

Choose the right lens color. One pair of polarized lenses is often not enough. Light-colored lenses allow you to see better in low light, and darker tints let you see better in bright sun. Amber is the most popular, all-around lens tint for freshwater fishing.

Fish at high noon. From 10 o'clock to 2 o'clock, the high overhead sun illuminates the streambottom, allowing you to easily see into the river.

Put the sun at your back so that you can see better, but be aware of your shadow.

Look for viewing lanes, places where you can see into the water without glare. Once you find a viewing lane, use it to scan the river.

Look for water windows. In broken, turbulent water, intermittent flat spots move downstream with the current. Look through these windows as they move downstream and scan the river bottom for fish.

Refine your approach. The best angle to spot fish is not necessarily the best angle from which to cast. Reposition yourself across or downstream from the fish after you've spotted it for the stealthiest approach. Once you reposition yourself, you may not be able to see the fish, so mark its location with something such as a stick on the bank or large rock on the bottom.

Know what to look for. Trout take on the color of their surroundings. Instead of looking for an entire fish, look for signs that betray their presence—shadows on the stream bottom, a waving tail, flashes as the fish feeds on nymphs, or certain species-specific features such as a brook trout's white-tipped fins or a rainbow's red sides.

White mouths. Flashes of white not only signal the presence of feeding fish, but when you are drifting a subsurface fly to a fish, the fish's white mouth is a good indication to strike—often before your indicator budges.

Look for feeding trout—they are the easiest to catch. Signs trout are feeding include rises, white mouths, flashes, and fish suspended in the water column. Trout hugging the bottom, fish not moving, or fish that are swimming away probably have lockjaw.

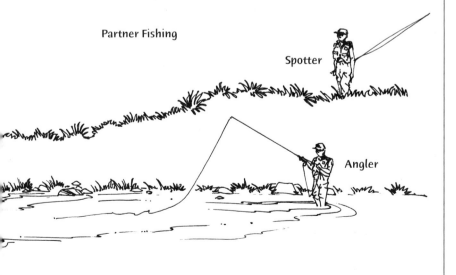

Partner Fishing

Spotter

Angler

TELLING TIME

Being able to communicate a fish's location to your partner is a critical skill when sight-fishing—whether on a spring creek or the flats.

Tell time when pointing out a fish to your partner. When you spot a fish, call out "fish," (or "tarpon," or "trout," whatever), and the caster points their rod straight ahead to establish 12 o'clock. (In a boat, the bow is always 12 o'clock and the stern is 6 o'clock.) Based on the rod tip (12 o'clock), the spotter calls out the location of the fish—9 o'clock would be 90 degrees left of the rod tip, 3 o'clock, 90 degrees right of the rod tip—and the distance and direction ("coming toward the boat," "going away," "moving left"), and the caster moves the rod tip. When the rod tip is pointing at the target, the spotter should call out the distance and direction again. The caster makes a presentation when they see the fish.

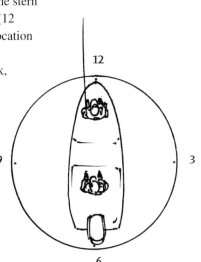

BE NOSY

When you spook a fish, watch where it goes. As long as you won't disturb other people's fishing, after you're done fishing a piece of water, walk through it and note where any spooked fish are and where they go.

WATCH YOUR FEET

When you step into the water, look at your wading shoes. The depth at which you can see your feet is more or less the distance at which a fish can see your fly. If there is just a few inches of visibility, fishing may be poor; 6 to 12 inches, it may be marginal and you should consider using flashy or bright-colored flies; more than 12 inches has promise; from 12 to 24 inches is still murky, but fishing can be good because the fish have less opportunity to inspect the fly. These are just guidelines. Every watershed is different.

HIGH, DIRTY WATER

Many hang it up when the water rises and gets cloudy, but fishing can be great if you know where to look.

Fish downstream of clear tributaries, or fish in the tributaries. Trout and steelhead often move upstream in high water.

Fish the Edges

Trout take a break from the current in backeddies and pockets of slower water near banks and behind structures. Fish these spots first.

Use brightly colored, large flies; if you swing flies downstream, you can cover more water to find the fish. Chartreuse and hot-pink colors are reliable fish catchers in murky water, as are black and purple because of their strong profile in dirty water.

Flies that make noise or push water are effective in slower water. Fish can key in on food with other clues rather than visual ones.

Spotting Saltwater Fish

Capt. John Kumiski

Fish betray their whereabouts in many ways. With a little practice and knowledge, it becomes easy to identify where they are. These tips are for finding popular Florida nearshore species, such as redfish, seatrout, tarpon, and jacks, but many are applicable for other saltwater species.

White spots. These are light-colored sandy areas on a bottom otherwise carpeted with grass. During cooler weather, seatrout and redfish lie on these white spots and sun themselves. Generally, you'll find more fish in an area with a bottom of mixed grass and sand than in areas of all grass or all sand.

Tailers. Redfish, black drum, and sheepshead sometimes feed in shallow water with their tails sticking out, a situation you always hope for.

Mullet schools. At certain times of the year, especially during the fall, the numbers of mullet are mind-boggling. Predators of all kinds shadow mullet schools. Mullet casually jump most of the time, allowing you to locate schools from afar, and when chased, leap frantically out of the water by the hundreds.

Waking fish. These are fish creating a wake as they swim through shallow water. They could be alone or in schools of hundreds. Redfish and jacks frequently do this, but other species such as bonefish and permit also push wakes.

Backing fish. Typically seen in the winter, these are waking redfish (singles or pairs) in shallow water with their backs exposed.

Finned-out fish. Schooling redfish in slick water often sun themselves, their dorsal fins periodically piercing the water's surface. Tarpon and jacks also do this.

Rollers. Tarpon porpoise on the surface to gulp air. You can hear them when they are close, and when the light is right, you can see them from a distance.

Wading birds. When you see several herons or egrets in the same area, stop and investigate. Bait is attracting the birds, and gamefish are often in the same area.

Diving birds. In the lagoons, ignore pelicans and cormorants. Gulls are marginal indicators, appearing most frequently over ladyfish. Terns almost always dive over jacks, trout, mackerel, or bluefish.

Tailers

4

Presentations

HOW TO BEAT DRAG

*Casts and other techniques to over-
come the current's pull on the fly*

Walk the Dog
On level stream bottoms and banks,
extend the drift of your fly by stepping downstream before it starts to
drag. Some anglers walk 20 feet or
so, but you can get a longer drift
with one or two steps and stretching
your rod arm downstream. Often,
this extra bit at the end is just the
ticket for tough trout.

Add Tippet
Though more difficult to cast, a
long tippet helps put critical S
curves in your leader that beat
micro drag.

Keep a Clean Line
When the tip of your floating line
sinks, the current pulls on the leader
butt and can ruin your drifts. A
clean line and a leader butt diameter
matched for your fly line ensure
your line tip floats high.

Minimize the Currents
Though not always possible, try to
reposition yourself to cast across as
few different currents as possible.
Upstream or downstream presentations make drag-free drifts easier
than across-stream presentations.

Don't Take Any Slack

Before you mend line, shake
out slack in front of you so
you don't pull slack out of the
line that you have cast. For the
same reason, when you make a
reach cast, have plenty of slack
line to shoot as you reach.

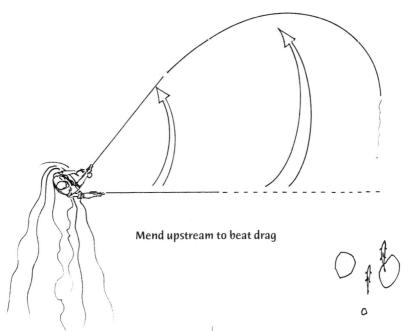

Mend upstream to beat drag

Mend

After you cast across stream, lift your line and place it upstream of the fly to slow down the current's pull on your line and leader.

If You Can't Beat Them, Join Them

In swirling eddies and other spots where it is impossible to get a good drag-free float, use flies that you can fish with an active retrieve, such as caddis dry flies or Woolly Buggers.

Keep Your Fly Line off the Water

When dry-fly fishing or nymphing in tricky currents, get close and keep as little fly line on the water as possible.

Learn the Stack Cast

The stack, or puddle, cast creates more slack line near the caster, which is helpful if you are standing in fast water and a trout is rising upstream in slower water. As with the parachute cast, aim past your target with excess line, and after you stop the rod, quickly drop the rod tip to the water, pulling the fly back to the target and creating a puddle of slack line on the water in front of you.

Learn the Reach Cast

A reach cast is especially helpful casting across stream when there are fast currents between you and your target. Cast at the target and just after the stop—while the line is still in the air—reach your rod and arm upstream and place the line in an arch. The current needs to remove this slack line before drag sets in. Combine a stack and reach cast for maximum drag-free drift.

Shock Absorber

With a dry-and-dropper rig, you can often mend your fly line and leader easily without it affecting the drift of the submerged fly. The dry fly floating on the surface may twitch a little, but it acts as a shock absorber in the system, preventing the nymph from moving much.

Boil Your Leader

Boil your leader butt sections for about 5 minutes to get the kinks and curls out and to make it more supple.

WATCH THE LINE

When casting to an upstream target, never let the line float downstream of your rod tip. If it does, you have too much slack to strike properly.

HANG OUT

At the end of a drift with a nymph, wet fly, or streamer, let the fly hang in the current for 20 to 30 seconds before picking up and casting again. Many fish strike when the fly is dangling directly downstream.

Cast Ahead of the Boat

With the fly quartered in front of the boat, you get a long drift. If you cast behind the boat, the fly will drag almost immediately, and you might be fishing in your partner's water. Use the oar as the dividing line.

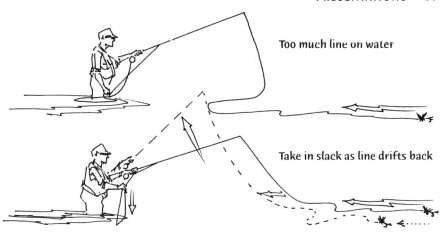

Too much line on water

Take in slack as line drifts back

DOWNSTREAM DRIFTS

To fish under brush and undercut banks, drift your fly downstream, feeding slack into the drift by popping the rod tip. You can often steer your fly left or right by mending line close to you.

DETERMINE DEPTH

The deeper the fish is holding, the farther upstream you should present your fly.

CREEP IT OUT

When your fly goes into the trees or mangroves, creep it out slowly and it will often fall gently into the water. Don't pull quickly or the fly is likely to wrap around a limb and make it difficult to retrieve. If your hook becomes stuck, a quick roll cast often frees the fly.

Watch the Currents

Fish do not always face upstream; they face into the current. Especially when fishing eddies, pay attention to the direction the water is moving and adjust your presentation accordingly. Foam, debris, or insects on the water can help you track the currents.

EASY-TO-SEE FLIES

A drab little dry may be a perfect match, but if you can't see your fly to set the hook or detect when it's dragging, it is of little use. Fish flies that you can see. Two flies—one indicator fly, one hatch-matcher—is another way to see what you are doing.

Kiwi Lessons

George Bisharat

Conveying advice from Martin Langlands, an independent guide based in Darfield, just outside Christchurch on New Zealand's South Island (troutlands.com).

If you spot, he's caught. Once you spot a fish, your chances of catching it soar. Watch the drift of your fly for accuracy, and set when the fish takes. Change patterns or presentation depending on the fish's reaction to your fly. Look for water that offers the best sight-fishing opportunities.

Drab gets the grab

Less is more. Short, straight casts of 30 feet or less minimize drag. Upstream casts where the fly line falls in a single current lane are particularly effective. Short-line casting is also more accurate.

After one perfect presentation without results, consider changing flies before trying again.

Stealth brings wealth. Wear drab, camouflage clothes and use drab-colored fly lines. Stay low—rod tip, too—and move slowly.

Wade quietly, and install a rubber tip on your wading staff (if you use one) or cover the end with duct tape to dampen the noise transmitted through the water.

Many Kiwis suggest not crossing upstream of a brown trout's lie because they feel that browns may smell pheromones we excrete in perspiration and skin oils—even through breathable waders—far from where we enter the stream.

Drab Gets the Grab

Drab-colored flies with dark bead heads outfish bright, shiny ones. New Zealand guides favor basic flies such as Hare's Ears, Pheasant Tails, and soft-hackles over garish, flashy patterns.

Buy or tie tungsten-bead flies. Tungsten is heavy and allows you to create fast-sinking flies with little material.

Dry-and-dropper rigs are a Kiwi mainstay, but guides use the smallest fly that floats the nymph. The dry fly is tied in the subtlest color still visible. Langlands ties the rig with 6 to 8 feet of 6-pound Maxima to the dry, then typically a tungsten beadhead nymph to the bend of the indicator fly with 3 to 6 feet of 2- or 3-pound Maxima, and then one more fly (often smaller and beadless) on 2- or 3-pound Maxima 4 to 6 inches off the bend of the second fly. This rig saves the expense of buying and time of building a tapered leader, which isn't necessary to turn over the flies.

Fearless Casters Catch More Fish

Use the structure. Bounce your dry flies off of rocks and cast bendbacks and other weedless flies to the bank or brush and pull them off. You may lose more flies, but there is often no other way to get your fly tight to the structure where the fish are holding.

Two-hand retrieve

TWO-HAND RETRIEVE

Borrow a tip from the salt: Tuck the rod up under your armpit and retrieve line with two hands for steady or fast streamer presentations. Sometimes fish want a fly that is constantly moving, which is hard to do with conventional stripping techniques.

BANKERS

When fishing terrestrials to trout hiding under the streambanks, don't cast too tight to the bank. Start a few feet off of the bank at first and work your fly closer on consecutive casts. This tactic prevents lining a fish, reduces drag (water next to the bank is generally flowing slower than the water on the outside of the fish), and gives the fish a chance to see the fly—it may not see the fly if you cast too close to the bank.

Bankers

SMALL-STREAM STRATEGIES
Look at Your Backcast
Look for open areas in the brush or trees, and aim your backcast through the hole. Knowing what is behind you is imperative in tight quarters, and good advice for all fly casting.

Cast Creatively
On many small streams, you won't have room for standard backcasts. Use Spey casts, bow-and-arrow casts, and water hauls to deliver your fly to the fish.

Fish the Leader
Most of the time, you'll be casting a short line and should just be fishing the leader, especially in pockets behind rocks and other tumbling currents.

Size Down, with Exceptions
Fish shorter rods, shorter leaders, and smaller line weights on small

Bounce cast

streams. Sometimes, longer rods are useful for dapping—poking a fly out through the brush and dancing it on top of the water with just the leader. To cast in tight quarters with a long rod, slide your casting hand up to a place just behind the stripping guide and brace the butt of the rod against your side. You just shortened your rod by a foot or so.

Fish Downstream

Often, this is the only way to drift your fly under banks and tight brush—where most of the fish are.

Cherry Pick

On small streams there are often barren areas not worthy of searching casts—don't waste your time in the extremely shallow riffles and barren runs. Concentrate on the best plunge pools and deep pockets. If you don't hook a fish quickly, move on.

Use Rocks

Cast over rocks, logs, and grass patches and let your line sit on them as you present your fly. Because your fly line isn't moving, you'll get longer drag-free drifts.

Mental Preparation

Frequent snags are part of the small-stream experience. If you can't handle this, and tangles, then fish more open water.

Cast Smarter

Hooking small fish spooks the larger ones. Identify the prime lies, and get your fly in there first.

Travel Light

You may have to cover lots of water and scramble over rocks. Stay nimble by only carrying fishing necessities: rod and reel, a few flies, floatant, extra tippet, and nippers.

Dapping with just the leader

NIGHT FISHING

Night fishing for trout, especially browns, is best when daytime water temperatures reach their highest. Also, major hatches of large insects such as Green and Brown Drakes or Hexagenia *bring up large fish, but usually under the cover of darkness. Across the country, aquatic moths, large stoneflies, and other giant morsels often emerge or lay eggs at night. Most anglers never see them, but the fish know they are there.*

Practice in the Dark
Practice casting during the day with your eyes closed to simulate fishing at night.

Know the Water
Explore the water, and your fishing spots, during the day. Don't fish strange water at night.

Fish the Shallows
Water too shallow for big trout during the day is often the best water to fish at night. Big browns love to prowl the shallows at night, and often chase minnows and slurp dry flies in the moonlight. Avoid the deep holes trout hide in during the day. At night, nearby tailouts and riffles at the heads of these deep pools are usually better bets.

Stay Late
Night fishing doesn't just mean staying out an extra hour after dark. The first hour of darkness is often a readjustment period for trout, and the best fishing doesn't get rolling until later. Fishing is also good in the early morning hours before and after sunrise—especially on busy rivers where 8 to 5 angler traffic and daytime heat puts the trout off.

Bring a Headlamp, but Use It Sparingly

Not only does the light spook fish, but it throws off your night vision, and your pupils have to readjust after you turn it off. When you turn on any light, turn away from water you are fishing.

Snook chase bait
attracted to dock lights

Rig Flies with Loops

Connect the fly to your tippet with your favorite knot. On the end of the tippet, tie a double surgeon's, perfection, or Kreh nonslip loop. Connecting these prerigged flies to your leader with a loop-to-loop when the light is low is a lot easier than threading tippet through the hook eye.

Fish Big Flies

Fish are often less picky about fly pattern at night. Fish larger flies with big white wings to help you see. Change to your night rig before it gets too dark to see.

Glow-in-the-Dark Lines

Some line manufacturers make glow-in-the-dark fly lines that don't seem to bother some species such as striped bass. Charge the line by exposing it to any light source, but for a quick charge, put it in a stripping basket, and fire a camera flash at it.

Feel It

Tie a nail knot with monofilament at the point in your fly line where you can comfortably pick up line to cast and load the rod. That way, you can always calculate the length of a straight cast as long as you know the length of your leader.

Use Heavy Tippets

Larger flies and less light mean heavier tippets. You'll also need to have heavier tippets to fight the fish quickly and from your position— you won't have the luxury of chasing a strong fish downstream. In the dark, the safest thing to do is to stand your ground and hope your tippet holds.

Watch the Wake

To help track your dry fly on moon-lit water, use a down-and-across presentation. After casting downstream, drag your fly into the fish's feeding lane, watching the reflection of moonlight off the small wake.

Dock Lights

Dock lights attract baitfish at night, which attracts everything from snook to stripers. In more urban trout-fishing environments, street and store lights can illuminate the water through the night, making it easy to see.

Carry Spare Lights

Always carry several sources of light, and spare batteries. Glow sticks are waterproof and good sources of backup light.

Mark Your Way

Carry white cloth strips (from an old T-shirt) and tie them around tree limbs or fences to mark your way out in the dark.

Spotlighting

Where legal, search the stream with a spotlight to locate large browns at night. Wait until you've fished a pool before bringing out the light.

STEALTH

Careful approaches catch more fish. Follow these basic rules.

Blend In

Wear clothes that are a color that match the environment in which you'll be fishing. Avoid reflective items, and when possible purchase gear with black or other nonreflective hardware.

Use the Shade

Approach from the shaded side of a bank to reduce the contrast between yourself and the bank, lessening the chances of spooking a fish.

Take a nap

Measure Twice

Carpenters say "measure twice, cut once." It's the same with casting to wary fish. Once you spot your target, measure out the line you think you'll need by letting it drift below you. Pick up and false-cast to the side of the fish, measuring the correct distance again, before your final presentation cast. Keep false-casting to a minimum.

Think Ahead

Fish the water closest to you first. Don't wade into a river without fishing the shoreline first. If floating a river (especially small rivers or in clear water) get out, walk downstream, and fish the good spots before drifting through them.

Approach from Behind

Not only can fish not see you, but the currents will dissipate waves and sound. This approach also generally gives you several tries at a fish, as long as you don't cast your fly line over it. The best position for stealth is behind and at a slight angle to your target.

Take Your Time

As you wade into the water, take the time to allow fish to adjust to your presence before you start casting. Once in the water, retie your leader, stretch your line, choose a new fly— anything to slow down. Often, fish will resume feeding after a short spell, and then you can cast to them with greater chance of success.

Don't Rip Line from the Water

Slowly lift your rod tip until the line is out of the water before beginning your backcast. Use a roll cast or snake roll to pick up your dry flies.

First Cast, Best Cast

Tough fish often don't give second chances. Make your first cast count.

Clear-Tip Lines

Fish in pressured areas spook when they see the fly line. With a clear-tip line, you essentially lengthen your leader the length of the clear tip—up to 15 feet. This is especially important on flats or in stillwaters where fish can swim toward the fly and fly line.

Sit Down

When fishing from a boat, try to sit if possible—you have a lower profile.

Take a Knee

Get down on one knee when casting from the bank. It helps you keep a low profile yet it's easy to get up and get moving again.

Don't Rock the Boat

When casting from a boat, especially in slower moving or still-waters, try not to move your body so much that you send wakes.

Match Movement to Water Speed

When fishing slow pools, move slowly. In faster water, you can get closer and move quicker. Let the fish tell you how close you can get to them. You may only have one shot at a big one, though, so err on the side of caution.

Cast Sidearm

A sidearm cast keeps the rod tip lower than an overhead cast—the rod might spook the fish—whether you are fishing for trout or bonefish.

Cast sidearm

Stillwater Trout

Brian Chan

Many fly fishers lack confidence when fishing lakes because they don't understand the underwater habitat or the sometimes-mysterious insect hatches. Solve the puzzle by learning about these key factors.

Watch the birds. Hatches are often confined to certain shoals (shallow-water zones) or specific locations. Birds, such as swallows, terns, gulls, and nighthawks, find emerging chironomids, mayflies, caddisflies, and other hatching insects quickly. Use binoculars to spot birds, particularly on bigger water.

Look into the water. Carry a small aquarium net to capture pupae, nymphs, emergers, and adult insects so you can match fly patterns to size and color. Place the specimens in a vial or white dish to get a better idea of color and to also watch the insects emerge.

Look on the water. Feeding trout leave distinct riseforms that provide clues to what insect stage they are eating. Trout feeding on minnows often show slashing rises as they work through the school of baitfish.

Look at bottom structure. Polarized sunglasses allow you to see better beneath the surface to spot shoals, drop-offs, spring areas, submerged trees, and bugs. You can find bottom-contour maps for many larger lakes, and if fishing in a boat or pontoon, a fish finder helps locate bottom structure.

Know your insects and other food sources. Learn to recognize the major aquatic invertebrate trout foods such as chironomids (midges), mayflies, caddisflies, damselflies, dragonflies, waterboatman, backswim-

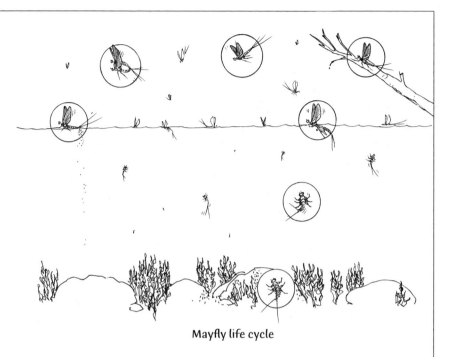

Mayfly life cycle

mers, scuds, leeches, snails, and forage fish. Equally important, learn about their individual life cycles and habitat requirements. Getting to know a particular lake or group of lakes translates into learning about the available food sources and knowing the emergence sequences peculiar to those individual waters. Many good reference books cover identification, life history, and distribution of the most common stillwater invertebrates. These insects' life cycles and emergence patterns are similar regardless of where a lake is geographically located—chironomids from a lake in the Northwest Territories emerge the same way as those in a nutrient-rich stillwater in southern New Mexico.

continued on page 54

Stillwater Trout continued

Learn about preferred food sources. Trout focused on a few dominant food sources in a lake can often become difficult to catch. Small nutrient-rich lakes often support immense chironomid and scud populations. Anglers that have consistent success in these waters have learned the details of the life cycles and habitat preferences of these preferred food sources. For instance, when chironomid pupae suspend just inches off the lake bottom, often for several days as they complete the transition from the larval to pupal stage, there can be great fishing even though the surface shows no sign of emergence.

Fly selection. Do some homework to learn what insects and other food sources live in stillwaters you will be fishing. Local fly shops, fly-fishing clubs, websites, and regional fishing guidebooks are good sources for this information. The ideal fly box has generic imitations of food sources plus some refined patterns that more closely imitate the various life stages of insects found specifically in those waters.

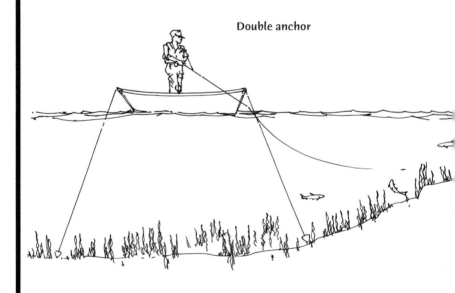

Double anchor

Water temperature matters. Water temperature influences the hatches, and each insect order has a preferred temperature range. The emergence sequence typically begins with midges, followed by mayflies, damselflies, caddisflies, and, lastly, dragonflies. The most intense emergences typically occur when surface water temperatures range between 50 and 65 degrees F.

In the spring, shallow areas—particularly areas with dark bottoms—warm first, and that's where the first hatches (usually midges) occur. Later in the summer, the same midge species hatch in deeper water, and the best fishing moves to these areas.

Choose the right fly line for the job. Be prepared to present flies from the surface to depths of up to 40 feet, depending on where fish are feeding.

Floating fly lines cover the shoal zone, water between 2 and 20 feet deep, and are required to present both floating and emerging imitations.

Slow or intermediate sinking lines are good for fishing water between 10 and 20 feet deep and allow you to fish pupal and nymphal patterns very slowly while ascending at a gradual angle toward the surface.

Fast or extra-fast sinking lines reach 15 to 40 feet and are useful for fishing dragonfly nymphs, leeches, and shrimp along the deeper edges or up the faces of drop-offs.

Proper boat setup. A stable flat-bottomed boat or pram is often the most effective way to fish lakes. In a hard-bottomed craft, you can stand up and look into the water and move from area to area much faster than a float tube. This can be critical when trying to locate specific insect emergences in a larger water body. Fishing out of a boat can be noisy, particularly if it is made out of aluminum. Reduce the chances of scaring fish by fitting outdoor carpeting over the boat floor. Sound travels fast in water, and trout have sensitive hearing systems.

Anchor system is key. It is critical to have anchors out both bow and stern, especially if two people are fishing from the same craft. Double anchoring prevents the boat from swinging back and forth when the

continued on page 56

Stillwater Trout continued

wind is constantly changing direction. A stationary boat allows the best control of fly lines and retrieves. It is important to have as straight a line connection between the fly rod, fly line, leader, and fly as possible so that you can detect even the softest bite. Simple anchor-control pulley systems make lifting, storing, and resetting anchors easy and require little movement within the boat.

Cover different depths

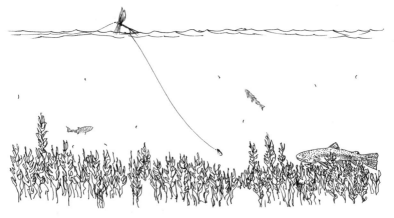

Explore and experiment. When exploring a new lake, slowly troll or drift and cast around the basin while getting a good look at shoals, drop-offs, weed beds, and other structure. Dragonfly nymphs and leeches are always good searching patterns. Both invertebrates are common inhabitants of lakes and both are big food items. Don't be afraid to try flashy or bright patterns like bead-headed Woolly Buggers, and frequently vary speed and direction when trolling or retrieving flies.

A Guide's Thoughts on Stealth and Presentations

Dave Ames

The top of your head is the part of you that trout see best: Don't wear brightly colored hats.

Sound travels five times faster in water than air. If you can hear yourself walking, you're wading too fast.

Informal studies conducted in my boat proved to me that when nymphing, fluorocarbon tippet caught about one-third more fish than traditional tippets.

Trout can smell certain amino acids in parts per trillion and people are made up of amino acids. Whatever you do, don't spit on your fly, especially if you're chewing tobacco.

Dead-drift your flies from a boat by casting slightly ahead of yourself in relation to the current. If you cast behind the boat, no matter how hard your guide is pulling on the oars, you won't get a drag-free drift.

If you're not catching any fish, stop. Smell the roses. Find a likely looking place and sit down for a while. Blend in. Watch the clouds. You'll be surprised how many times you'll look back to the river and find yourself surrounded by rising trout.

Mend, Don't Cast

When fishing weighted nymphs the best cast is the one you don't make. Leave the fly (or flies) in the water and give them time to sink. If it takes your flies five seconds to sink down to the fish, and you make another cast every five seconds, the fish will never see your flies. Extend that drift as far as possible by mending instead of making another false-cast.

5

Catching and Releasing Fish

MATCH HOOK SET TO CURRENT SPEED

Slow water generally means slow rises—wait to set the hook. Fast water equals fast rises—be quick on the draw.

SLOW RISERS

Large trout also rise slowly. Don't set the hook until you see the fly disappear, or you may pull the fly away from a willing trophy. British anglers are taught to say "God save the queen" before striking. Small trout strike quickly and often hook themselves.

ROLL-CAST STRIKE

If you are fishing upstream, it's often a good idea to raise your rod tip as the line comes back to you so you don't pull out the S curves in your line. If a fish strikes with your rod tip high, roll cast to set the hook, or snap the rod tip down sharply.

STRIP-STRIKE

When streamer fishing, strike by stripping line rather than hauling back on the rod tip, which often pulls the fly out of the water and spoils any other attempts the fish might make for your fly. When

Roll-cast strike

nymph fishing, you also don't want to pull the fly out of the water when you strike. To set when nymphing, gently pull the slack out of the line. If you detect a fish, set the hook with a short strip-strike. If not, leave your fly in the water.

NYMPH ON EDGE

The best nymph anglers are twitchy and set the hook at every strange movement of the indicator. Don't wait for the indicator to plunge underwater before you set.

LONG-LINE STRIKE

If you are dry-fly fishing or nymphing with a lot of line out, haul back on the rod and simultaneously strip line with your other hand to quickly take up all the slack and set the hook.

Go Light, Go Barbless

If you tie your own flies, consider tying nymphs and other subsurface patterns on light-wire hooks—if they hold the size of fish you typically catch. Thin-wire hooks penetrate more easily than heavy-wire hooks. Barbless hooks penetrate more easily than barbed ones.

DO NOTHING

When dry-fly fishing for steelhead or Atlantic salmon, don't set the hook until you feel the fish's weight bend the rod. All too often, jittery anglers set the hook—as they were taught to do for other species—and pull the fly from the fish's mouth.

FIGHTING FISH

HAVE A PLAN

Before casting to a fish or to where you suspect a fish might be holding, have a plan for how you'll hook, fight, and land it. Often, a hooked fish swims toward nearby structure. Determine the best angle from which to get the necessary leverage to pull the fish away.

GET A SCALE

A few minutes pulling with your rod on a fly line attached to a Chatillion scale will teach you most of what you need to know about how to apply pressure with a fly rod. Practice with the most common tippet sizes that you use and teach yourself how hard you have to pull before you break the tippet. You'll be amazed at how little pressure you can actually apply with a fly rod.

KEEP THE ROD LOW

This goes along with the scale exercise. If you just flex the rod tip by lifting up, you cannot exert much pressure. Keep the rod tip low and to the side and fight the fish from the butt.

AVOID JERKS

Jerks break line, not (generally) steady pulls. Do this simple exercise: Pull slowly and steadily on 4X tippet until it breaks, then jerk it. Remember this when you are fighting fish.

MANAGE SLACK

Play all but the smallest fish from the reel. If the fish is strong enough to pull excess slack line through the guides, let it do so. This helps get it on the reel quickly. However, managing slack line is always top priority, so if the fish runs toward you, strip line to stay tight, and worry about reeling later.

Take a bow

REEL DOWN TO RECOVER LINE

Fight the fish with the rod, and reel down as you recover line. This holds true for everything from trout to tarpon. Reeling down means reeling while you recover the line you've taken back from the fish as you bring the rod back down low to begin pumping again.

JUST RELAX

Sometimes when a large fish buries itself into weedbeds or brush, you can relax pressure on the fish and it will swim back to the spot where you hooked it.

HANDS OFF

Never grab the reel handle when a fish—any fish—is taking off line. Large fish can run so fast, the spinning handle will smash your knuckles. Hands in the way of the reel handle can break off any fish by preventing line from going out.

Have High Hopes

Rig with tackle and tippet matched to the largest fish you expect to catch so you can land the fish as quickly as possible.

TAKE A BOW

If any fish jumps—tarpon or trout—lower the rod tip to put slack in the line. This is called "bowing" in tarpon-fishing lingo, but it's equally important for large trout, salmon, and steelhead.

AVOID WARM WATER

The warmer the water, the less you should play and handle trout. Fish elsewhere if water temperatures exceed 70 degrees F. Playing a trout in those warmer temperatures stresses it too much. Find colder water or fish for warmwater species.

Fight at Right Angles

Move the rod tip from side to side to disorient and quickly tire a fish. Pull at right angles to the fish's head.

SMOOTH CONNECTIONS

Keep the leader outside of the rod tip when landing a fish to prevent the line-to-leader knot from snagging on your guides. If you are fishing a long leader and you need to bring the line and leader connection inside of the rod tip and into the guides, make sure that you use a smooth line-to-leader connection such as a needle knot coated with Pliobond or a Zap-A-Gap splice. If not, the connection can catch on a guide and break if the fish makes a last-effort run.

GET INTO POSITION

The best position to fight a trout is from across or downstream of it. The fish works against the current and you pull the hook into the fish's mouth. The riskiest position is if you hook a fish straight downstream of you. If this happens, get below it to fight and land it, even if you have to back out of the water, get on dry land or in shallower water, and walk swiftly downstream. It's always easier to pull a fish in if you aren't battling it and the current.

Bring a fish downstream into the net

RELEASING FISH

GO BARBLESS

Barbless hooks make releasing fish easier and are also easier to unsnag from nets, clothing, and flesh.

If you forget to pinch down the hook barb before fishing, you can still do it while releasing a fish. Push the hook through all the way so the barb is exposed, pinch it down with hemostats or needle-nose pliers, and back the hook out.

HANDS OFF

Always try to keep the trout in the water while releasing it. As you bring the fish in, grasp the fly with your fingers or forceps and twist to release the fish without touching it.

HANDLING FISH
Tail It

If you have to handle the fish, grasp it at the base of the tail (after you've wet your hands) or wear a tailing glove or damp cloth to help you get a grip. Cradle the fish with your other hand and never squeeze or apply pressure to the belly where the vital organs are located.

Upside Down

A calm fish is easier to handle than one flopping all over the place. Immobilize small fish by holding them upside down (out of the water).

Upside down

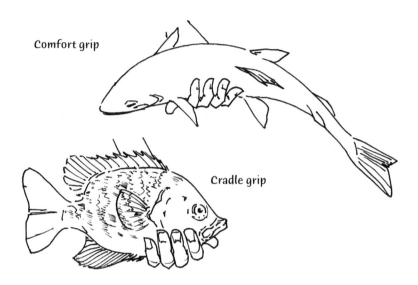

Comfort grip

Cradle grip

Comfort Grip

Use the comfort grip to pick up larger fish. Slide your hand underneath the center of the fish's weight, usually a few inches behind the head. Then lift the fish slowly. Spread your hand to balance the fish.

Cradle Grip

Cradle spiny fish such as panfish by their bellies to avoid getting stuck.

Hold Your Breath

Don't hold fish out of the water longer than you can hold your breath.

HELPING HAND

If the fish doesn't swim away quickly, Lefty Kreh recommends the following: grasp its lower jaw with your thumb, which helps to open the fish's mouth. Gently rock the fish back and forth in the water so that the oxygen-rich water goes over the fish's gills. Release the fish only after it swims from your grasp.

Revive a fish by holding it head-first into gentle current. Release fish in slower moving (but not silty) water. Hold the fish steady until it maintains itself upright. If you are in a boat, row to slower water to release the fish.

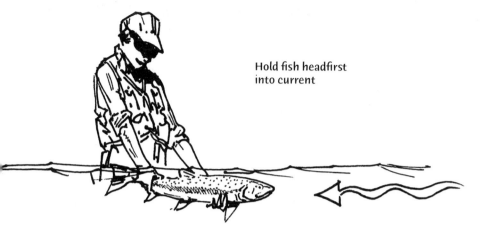

Hold fish headfirst
into current

KEEP COOL

In the summer, many slow
shallow areas or backwaters are
much warmer than the main current.
Do not release trout in these areas.
When water temperatures are high,
release trout near the main current
where the water is cool and well
oxygenated.

CUT THE TIPPET

If the fish has swallowed the fly
deeply, cut the tippet. The fly will
generally shake free or dissolve over
time, and you can do more damage
by trying to extricate the hook.

USE RUBBER-MESH NETS

Avoid cotton or nylon mesh nets. If
you use a net, use one of the newer,
rubber ones. You'll get fewer tangles with your tandem-fly rigs and
it's easier on the trout.

Old nylon net

Newer
rubber net

HANDLING AND RELEASING FISH BY SPECIES

First try to unhook all of these fish with forceps or pliers, keeping the fish in the water to prevent handling.

Species	Watch Out For	Notes
Fresh Water		
bluegill, sunfish, rock bass	sharp spikes on fins	cradle fish, cupping belly
catfish	sharp dorsal and pectoral spines can inflict painful, venomous wounds	slide up from the tail with your thumb on the belly and place first pectoral fin between thumb and forefinger and dorsal between the forefinger and middle finger and let ringfinger come up behind left pectoral fin so all the fins are poking out between fingers
trout (all species)	sensitive organs, teeth on larger fish	cradle belly with cupped hands, use two hands for larger fish (one behind head, the other behind tail); stabilize in gentle currents to release
bass (smallmouth and largemouth)	damaging fish's jaw when you "lip" it	"lip" fish by grasping its lower jaw with your thumb and forefinger; keep it vertical or support the tail if you turn it horizontally
musky and pike	sharp teeth	hold fish behind the head and use long-handled pliers to remove fly
steelhead and salmon	sensitive organs	tail fish with a glove or tailing mit by grasping the thick part (wrist) in front of the tail; avoid beaching fish to land them

HANDLING AND RELEASING FISH BY SPECIES

Species	Watch Out For	Notes
Salt Water		
barracuda (and wahoo)	sharp teeth; fish often leap near boat	release a large fish by cutting the wire with pliers as near to the mouth as possible; grasp smaller fish behind the head with gloved hands and take the hook out with pliers
bluefish	sharp teeth	use long-handled pliers to remove fly
bonefish	sharks following in a hooked fish	revive thoroughly so it doesn't become shark food
cobia	8 to 10 sharp spines in front of the dorsal fin	cobia can retract these spines so you may not see them
false albacore	releasing fish properly requires launching it headfirst into the water	grab fish by the bony area in front of the tail (gloves help)
permit	crushers in throat	revive thoroughly so it doesn't become shark food
redfish	strong crushers in mouth; sharp gill rakers	to handle, hold fish behind head and pinch gill covers together
shark	teeth; fish can bite even when "dead"; can bend head back to its tail to bite you; rough skin	large sharks should never be brought inside the boat; cut leader to release
snook	sharp gill covers	hold fish horizontally with hands under belly and on tail
stripers	sharp gill rakers, sandpaper-like teeth	use a glove to lip smaller fish to save wear and tear on your fingers
tarpon	large fish are dangerous near or in the boat	leave fish in the water and grab the lower jaw with a gloved hand to remove a hook; ensure fish is tired enough to minimize thrashing (which can be dangerous if it's a 100-pound fish) but thoroughly revive it before swimming away so it isn't vulnerable to sharks

Better Fishing Photography

Barry and Cathy Beck

A photograph captures and records a moment in time. Photographs tell stories, and good photographs create a sense of visual awareness that have an impact on the viewer. Be creative and use your imagination when you compose your pictures. Remember, in the end, beauty is in the eye of the beholder.

Remember to bring your camera. You can't take pictures without it. Make sure that your batteries are fully charged. You won't believe how many of our friends show up with a camera full of dead batteries. Bring along an extra memory card or extra film—you can't buy them on the stream.

Use existing light to your best advantage. Sunlight coming over the photographer's shoulder or from the side almost always works best to light your subject.

Compose your image carefully before you press the shutter. Keep the horizon straight and look for distracting background and foreground objects. If your subject is an angler holding a fish, make sure the angler looks happy.

Hold your camera still before you gently squeeze the shutter button. Use a monopod, tripod, or brace your elbows against your body to help keep the camera stable. Camera shake gives you fuzzy pictures.

Don't remove the hook when photographing someone holding a fish, until after you have taken the picture. If the fish escapes and the fly is still in its mouth, it can be landed and photographed again. Otherwise it's good-bye fish and no picture. Believe us, it happens.

Capture the moment. Take more than one picture of your subject. This is important because we all blink and no one wants a picture with a person with their eyes closed. **Take both vertical** and horizontal pictures. You might like one format better than the other. **Use flash to remove** unwanted shadows. The fill-flash mode in your camera is one of the most useful tools you have.

Like your polarized sunglasses, a polarizing filter on your camera lens not only eliminates glare from the water surface but also helps cut the reflective glare from the side of a fish. Fish scales often reflect light that overexpose your image.

Handling tips. Fish can be slippery and hard to hold. A firm grip around and just in front of the tail with the other hand gently cradling the underside of the fish near the pectoral fins works well. Keep the fish underwater until you have composed the picture and are ready to press the shutter. Then ask the subject to lift the fish out of the water long enough to take the photo. Release the fish carefully, making sure it has recovered. Keep the fish underwater between photographs.

WEIGHING IN

Measure length (in inches) from the tip of the fish's nose to the fork of the tail. Measure girth at the widest part of the fish's body. Use a flexible measuring tape or piece of string. Average girth equals half the length of a steelhead or trout.

ROUGH WEIGHT

If the fish is between 25 to 35 inches, you can get a rough weight by subtracting 20 from the length—a 35-inch steelhead of average girth is approximately 15 pounds.

NET WEIGHT

If you carry a Boga Grip, don't attach it directly to the mouth of a trout, salmon, or steelhead to weigh it. Instead, place the fish in a net and weigh the fish and the net, subtracting the net's weight from your total.

MAKESHIFT RULERS

For easy measuring aids, many anglers measure their hand span, the distance from finger tip to elbow (for larger fish), mark measurements on their rod or wading staff, or use a familiar object. A one-dollar bill is approximately 6 inches.

KEELIN ESTIMATOR

Tom Keelin (flyfishingresearch.net) says standard formulas underestimate a salmon, steelhead, or trout's weight. The formula he proposes reads: Fish weight (lbs) = length x (girth x girth) / 690, where length is measured from the tip of the nose to the fork of the tail in inches, and girth is measured at its largest point in inches. Keelin derived the 690 formula based on physical measurement of length, girth, and weight of 87 steelhead caught and released during 2001–2006 from the Babine and Kispiox rivers in British Columbia, Sandy River in Alaska, and other rivers.

PIKE AND MUSKY

Length x length x length / 3,500

TROUT, SALMON, AND STEELHEAD
Length x (girth x girth) / 800

BASS
Length x length x girth / 1,200

SUNFISH AND CRAPPIE
Length x length x length / 1,200

PART 2

Equipment

6

Flies and Hooks

DRY FLIES

Save time on-stream and pretreat your dry flies with your favorite floatant at home.

Albolene, the facial cleanser, makes a good dry-fly treatment. Melt it in a pan inside another pan filled with water. Let the water come to a rolling boil and stir the Albolene until it liquifies. Pour into a small container.

Think outside of the tube. Some anglers report success with nontraditional floatants such as clear silicone grease (for lubing O rings) available at hardware stores. Others

say beeswax mixed with Everclear (alchohol) makes a natural, biodegradable fly floatant, and lip balm (such as Chapstick or Carmex) works well in a pinch.

Make your own desiccant with Fletch Dry, a fine silica powder used for archery. Put it in a small container and apply it with a small paintbrush. Anglers also report good success with hydrophobic fumed silica used to gel and thicken epoxies, which may be the same stuff.

Watch the weather. In cold weather, keep gel fly floatants warm in a pocket close to your body so they flow smoothly. In summer, these gels pour out fast, so open the cap with the bottle upright and don't squeeze the bottle too hard.

Scotchguard

Several light applications of Scotchguard (the one with the green cap for outdoor fabrics) waterproofs your flies. Spray flies in batches and allow to dry overnight.

Different Fly
Treatments

Powder   Gel   Liquid

Dump out and store half of your powder desiccant (like Frog's Fanny) for the future. If you carry a small amount (only as much as you need for a few trips), it won't *all* blow away in a strong wind.

Apply paste first on your fingertips, and then use your fingertips to apply the dressing on the fly. Carry a small rag or handkerchief to blot your fly and remove excess dressing so you don't have little oil slicks around your fly. False-casting a few times helps fluff out the feathers.

Never put oil or paste on a soggy fly because you'll only seal in the wetness. Dry the fly with a rag or piece of amadou and then draw out the rest of the moisture with a dessi-cant. Silicone and paste-type floatants are only for dry flies that can absorb the treatment.

Microwave Shimizake and other products with silica crystals on high for approximately 20 seconds to revive (dry out) the treatment.

SMALL FLIES

Small flies tangle in a compartment fly box, making it difficult to pick a fly without removing a clump of them. Insert each fly into ripple foam, slotted foam, or on a magnet strip. You can make your own boxes with magnets for small flies. Stick them in the foam with tweezers so that you don't crush the hackles.

Hold the hook

Hold the hook bend of a small fly with forceps when you tighten the knot.

Cut tippet at an angle with sharp nippers before threading it through the eye of a small fly. Biting it smashes and flattens the tippet, making it harder to thread through the eye of a small fly.

Tie small flies on wide-gap, heavy-wire hooks to keep large fish on the line. You can also tie small flies on larger hooks to have more holding power. Fish sometimes ignore an oversized hook if what is tied on the hook matches the naturals.

Add a section of Powergum to your leader butt with a double uni knot to protect light tippets, especially with faster-action rods.

Buy magnifying eyeglasses at the drugstore for tying on small flies. They are inexpensive, so buy several and keep a spare in your vest or pack.

Treat the wing of a small dry fly with a white desiccant powder like Frog's Fanny, which helps you see your fly as it's getting dark.

Grease the leader with floatant up to 12 inches away from the dry fly. The greased, floating section of leader reflects light and is easy to see and use as a strike indicator.

Fish a larger, easier-to-see dry fly in front of a small dry fly or nymph (attach the smaller fly to the bend of the indicator fly) or add a bit of strike putty to the leader in front of it.

TANDEM TIPS

Wrap pretied tandem rigs around a piece of pipe insulating foam or store them in envelopes to save time on-stream.

Balance your dry fly with your nymph in a dry-and-dropper rig—if your nymph is too heavy it can sink your dry fly.

Charles Meck ties loops into his dry flies and nymphs so that he can easily attach his flies to his leader with a loop-to-loop connection.

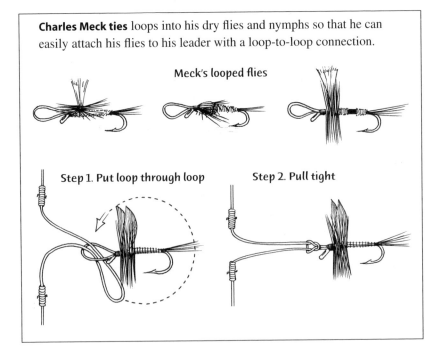

Meck's looped flies

Step 1. Put loop through loop

Step 2. Pull tight

Bicycle Rig

When fishing multiple flies, use different phases of the insect that is hatching to cover more bases, such as a dun and nymph or nymph and emerger.

Fish larger fly

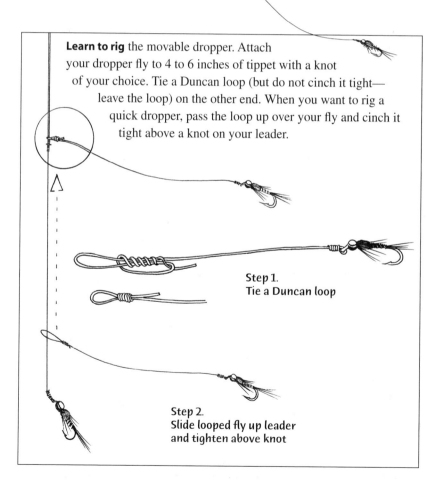

Learn to rig the movable dropper. Attach your dropper fly to 4 to 6 inches of tippet with a knot of your choice. Tie a Duncan loop (but do not cinch it tight—leave the loop) on the other end. When you want to rig a quick dropper, pass the loop up over your fly and cinch it tight above a knot on your leader.

Step 1.
Tie a Duncan loop

Step 2.
Slide looped fly up leader
and tighten above knot

Nymphing without Indicators

Jim McLennan

Indicators make nymphing easy, but on some heavily fished streams, conditioned fish stop feeding when they see them.

Large indicators can create a large disturbance on the water when they land. In flat water, you may be better off greasing part of the leader with fly floatant so that it floats high and is visible. Watch it for any movement to detect strikes.

Without an indicator, you can control the depth of your fly manually with your rod tip. When water depth varies greatly, as it does near boulders and in pocket water, the fixed depth provided by a strike indicator becomes a handicap. Because it's annoying to constantly adjust your indicator, most people don't do it, and either fish over trout's heads most of the time or just fish water suited for their rig.

Leaders without indicators slice through the surface currents, allowing the nymph to drift at the proper speed near the stream bottom. Because surface currents are faster than bottom currents, an indicator tends to pull the subsurface fly along the bottom unnaturally fast.

Indicators don't indicate every time a fish strikes, or by the time they do twitch, the fish has spit out the fly. Fish without an indicator, and you'll learn to look into the water for signs of a take—a white mouth, a flash.

Fashion a built-in strike indicator by attaching a short length of Amnesia to your fly line to use as a leader butt and tie a perfection or nonslip loop to the end of it.

NYMPHS

Add Frog's Fanny floatant to your nymph to simulate the air bubble on an emerging natural.

Color code your nymphs by weight with tying thread if you tie your own. Alternatively, use different types of beads with different sink rates to cover different depths more effectively. Tungsten sinks faster than brass.

Thin-profile flies with few materials sink faster than bulky nymphs with legs and hackle.

The thinner the tippet diameter, the faster the nymph sinks.

With some split shot, you can fish any dry fly as a nymph. Carry scissors for on-stream modifications.

If a fish refuses your dry fly, lengthen your leader, go down in tippet size, or change to another drabber and perhaps smaller surface fly.

Velcro Effect

One reason shaggy flies like Hare's Ears work so well is that they catch on a fish's teeth, preventing them from spitting out the fly quickly.

Often, the best method is to follow with a sunk fly (either in the surface or jut below). Fish seem to be less apprehensive about taking a fly in the water than one on the water.

STREAMERS
Cover the Water

Streamers and other swung wets are effective because you can cover a lot of water with them. The easiest way to fish a streamer is downstream. This allows you to swing your fly and step down after a drift, so that you can cover a lot of water without having to wade against the current.

Mimic the Bait

Most baitfish swim and feed with their heads facing into the current, so a presentation that brings the fly across and upstream is usually the best.

Tandem streamer

Tandem Streamers

Fish two streamers to cover more bases. Make sure you vary the patterns, though. Fish one light and one dark fly, one large and one small fly, or two different styles of streamers.

Beat Drag

Eddies that wreak havoc on your dead-drifting dry fly are perfect spots for streamers. Because you fish them on an active retrieve, drag isn't a factor.

Use Heavy Tippet

Fish see the fly first, so they won't spook from the tippet, and the stout tippet will help you pull your fly free from brush and other tangles

Match the Bottom

Many insects and baitfish can camouflage themselves to match their habitat, so try and match the overall color of the stream bottom when choosing a streamer or nymph.

that undoubtedly will trap your fly when casting toward shore.

Bendbacks

Bucktail bendbacks are practically weedless and allow you to cast onto the bank and pull your fly off, one secret of anglers who catch lots of fish. Bendbacks are an old, and often forgotten, fly style tied on hook bent to ride point up.

Bendback

Hang Out

Let your streamer hang in the currents for a bit and twitch it straight upstream, instead of picking it up immediately after it comes around on the swing. Fish will often hit a streamer fished in this manner when they won't hit it any other way.

Last Cast

At night, after you've fished the rise, try fishing streamers. Large trout and bass often feed on the baitfish feeding on insects. Plus, you don't have to watch the streamer when you fish it. The hits will be hard enough you won't have a problem detecting strikes.

Look to the Salt

Use small saltwater baitfish patterns for trout and bass. Saltwater fly tiers are masters at re-creating baitfish—it's what most of them do best. Just because a fly isn't marketed as a trout pattern doesn't mean that you can't use it or modify the design to imitate local baitfish species. Saltwater anglers also gave trout fishers the two-handed retrieve (see page 44), which is deadly for fish that want a steadily retrieved fly.

Match Tackle to Fly Size

Large browns frequently eat fish that exceed 6 inches, though trout anglers rarely cast patterns half that size. To catch big trout, don't be afraid to fish large flies and use tackle that makes casting larger patterns easy. Use 6- or 7-weight rods for large streamers.

Nymph It

Dead-drift a streamer like a nymph. Drifting streamers imitate crippled baitfish and are a change of pace for trout on pressured fisheries grown weary of watching stripped streamers.

Strip In-Line

When retrieving streamers, move your rod hand to the same side of your body as your stripping hand. This minimizes the angle of pull against your stripping finger and reduces friction.

Rod Tip Low

Always keep the rod tip low to the water and pointed at the fly when stripping streamers.

Instant Conehead

Make any streamer sink deeper by slipping a tungsten cone on the leader before attaching the fly. You can also use beads. Works for nymphs, too.

Instant conehead

Drift-Boat Streamer Tactics

Jim McLennan

Fishing streamers from a boat is one of the most effective tactics for catching large trout. Because you can control your drift and are positioned to cast toward the bank, many guides get their clients throwing streamers when nothing is hatching.

Bombing the banks works any time of year as long as the fish are there, but prime time is while the river is receding and clearing from spring runoff. The high velocity pushes fish out of the heavy midriver flows where they concentrate along sheltered banks. Cloudy water promotes aggressive feeding. I look for at least 18 inches of visibility.

In low, clear flows, fish usually move off the banks, hold in deeper water during the day, and return to the bankside shallows at night. Float early in the morning to get to the trout before the high sun forces them to retreat to deeper water, or pound the banks with streamers as you drift toward the takeout after an evening of dry-fly fishing.

For bombing the banks, look for water 2 feet or deeper near the bank with medium to quick flow. Target banks with structure such as boulders, deadfall, and deflections that block or constrict current and create current seams.

Look Ahead

If two people are fishing, they must keep their casts more or less parallel to avoid tangles. It's best to look ahead to the next good spot rather than look back to the previous one.

During the retrieve, keep the rod tip low so each strip moves the fly. Follow the streamer with the rod tip, and mend as needed to keep the line as straight as possible between the rod tip and the fly. If your cast lands with slack in the line, quickly make several long strips to remove it so the fly moves as soon as possible.

Vary Your Retrieve

Try long, short, quick, and slow strips, mixed with tantalizing twitches of the rod tip. When you get a strike, try to remember what you were doing, and repeat it.

Where trout hold in pockets near fast water, retrieve the fly just a short distance before casting again. Trout rarely chase a streamer out into heavy current.

In slower water, fish sometimes follow the fly a considerable distance, so retrieve it up to the boat.

To land a large trout from a drifting boat, move the boat to slower water along the shore or the inside of a bend. If you want to get a photo, get out of the boat and land the fish using a soft-mesh or rubber-mesh net.

If you hook a fish in fast water, plan to play it from the boat until you drift into slower water. If you're required by law or circumstances to land a fish from the boat, use a long-handled net with a nonabrasive rubber bag. Leave the fish in the net while you unhook it and row (keeping the fish in the water) to slower water to release it.

Look for trout in deeper water when the water near the banks is too shallow, too warm, or too cold, or when the water is clear and the sun is bright. Heavy boat pressure can also chase them from shallow bankside lies to deeper water.

In deep water, try dead-drifting (with some twitches) your streamer slow and deep through current seams. Have the oarsman slow the boat to half the current's speed, cast upstream at a 45-degree angle toward the seam, and as soon as the fly lands, mend upstream. With the rod tip low, follow the fly downstream. Retrieve it in slow strips to stay in touch with the fly, and make additional mends to keep the fly moving slow and deep as it gradually catches up to and passes the boat. This method works best with a sinking-tip line but also works with a floating line and a weighted fly in medium-depth water.

HOOKS

SHARPENING HOOKS

Check Your Point

When you get several hits but fail to hook up, check your hook point. Also frequently check your hook if you are nymphing and ticking the bottom a lot.

Old fish hook

Thumbnail Test

Hold the hook's point at about a 45-degree angle and slowly drag it down your thumbnail. If the point catches, it's sharp.

Carry a Hook Hone

Touch up small trout flies with an inexpensive diamond-dust fingernail file common in most department stores and pharmacies.

Sharpening Stone

Smooth streamside rocks make adequate hook hones in a pinch. Pull the hook point against the flat face of a rock, rotate, and repeat.

Debarb At Home

Crush the barb before you get to the stream. Use flat-faced pliers or forceps, and mash the barb in line with the hook point, not perpendicular, so you don't stress and weaken the point. Crimp barbs before tying flies on the hooks because you always run the risk of damaging a hook while debarbing and you don't want to waste a fly.

Debarb properly

STAYING SHARP

With modern chemically sharpened hooks, most trout anglers never sharpen a hook. But you may have to touch up your hook in the field. Some saltwater and warmwater anglers still use stainless-steel hooks that require sharpening. Specialty hones are available (and come with instructions), but many pros use common files. Here are three time-tested methods of sharpening a hook with a file.

Touch Up

This method is often rec-ommended by manufac-turers of chemically sharpened hooks, which generally come sharp out of the box and only need touch-ing up if they become dull from hooking a hard-mouthed fish or ticking bottom. You aren't cutting an edge on the hook, just honing an existing one. With the hook in a vise or your forceps, lightly push the whetstone or file from the point toward the barb. Repeat this step, going around the point. In a pinch, you can use this method with smooth stones, emery boards, and matchbox covers.

Touch up

File toward the Bend

If you file toward the point, the point can roll to one side. File both sides and then the bottom to form a triangle point.

Triangulation Method

Put the hook in a vise or in a pair of forceps. With a diamond-dust file (for small hooks) or a flat file (for saltwater and streamer hooks), file between the point and the barb on the inside of the hook point (between the point and the shank) toward the hook bend at about a 30-degree angle. (Look for the angle of the existing edge and try to match that.) Do the other side at the same angle. Touch up the outside of the hook point by filing it flat, so that you form a triangle shape.

Bob Clouser's method for stain-less-steel saltwater and bass hooks is a slight variation of the triangulation method. Clouser only files the two inside parts of the hook at an angle and leaves the bottom (opposite the barb) and the top (barb side) alone. After crimping down the barb, he places the hook in the vise upside down, so that he is facing the hook point. He recommends three swipes toward the hook bend on each side of the hook point with a flat metal file (fine). For trout hooks, you can use a diamond-dust file.

Diamond Point Method

Lefty Kreh favors this method for saltwater hooks.

Hold the hook upright and by the bend in a vise or pair of vise grips. The goal is to create four equally angled sides so that the hook looks like a pyramid when viewed straight on. Make the first angle by holding the file at 45 degrees and make a few smooth strokes toward the hook bend. Always move the file from the hook point to the bend. On large hooks, pass the file from the near side of the shank to the far side of the barb. Stroke the file at the same angle on the other side of the hook to form a triangle.

Invert the hook in the vise and repeat the process on both sides of the bottom of the hook. Sharpen only a small portion of the hook point. A long, tapered point is weak and can break.

Diamond Point

Step 1

Step 2

Approximate angle

Front view of sharpened hook

FLY BOXES

PURGE STALE PATTERNS

Organize your fly boxes and replenish stock in the off-season. Make your fly choice more efficient by simplifying the number of flies you carry. Get rid of flies you never use and only keep your top patterns. That way, you don't waste time onstream pondering fly choice.

GRAB AND GO

Keep separate boxes for separate fish species, different rivers, or different seasons or insect hatches so that you can grab and go without reorganizing your flies. Label the outsides for quick reference.

STREAMER SLEEVES

Lefty Kreh, Bob Clouser, and others store their streamers in plastic sleeves and then organize them in one of the folding, soft-sided spinnerbait bags available from several tackle shops. This is a great way to organize streamers that are

Tie or Buy in Bulk

Tie or buy flies by the half-dozen (many recommend by the dozen). Don't stock your boxes with singles. Not only is this a recipe for a disorderly box, you'll want more than one of a fly that works.

too large for conventional boxes and makes it easy to put a few in your pocket or fanny pack in case you need them. Plastic sleeves are available in bulk from Chiswick.com and other suppliers.

BUDGET BOXES

Transform any box into a fly box with hot glue (or other type of glue) and craft-store foam. Magnetic tape also works well in a box, especially for midges and other small patterns. This is the perfect way to ship a gift of flies.

Budget boxes

Wash and Dry

You can restore flies by wetting them, placing them in a colander, and blowing them with a hair dryer.

VHS FLY BOXES

Make your fly boxes out of old VHS tape boxes. Hot-glue 3mm foam on each side in sheets or thin strips of thicker, 5mm foam. These store easily on shelves or in boat bags. Label the case's spine for quick reference.

TAME LOOSE FLIES

Some manufacturers sell replacement fly-box ripple foam with adhesive backing. Cut it to size and stick it on the visor or dash of your fishing car or the inside of your boat to tame loose flies. These adhesive-backed foam fly patches are also handy in drift and pontoon boats.

CLEAR EYES

Check the eyes of all your flies at home, in good light, so you don't have to fuss with them when the fish are rising.

Heat a needle and poke it through the eye or clear it with a pin or bodkin. Lacquer can be fixed, but if the eyes are blocked by thread, either throw the fly out or don't buy it in the first place.

Cauterizing tools also work well for clearing epoxy out of the eyes of larger flies and are handy to have around the tying bench for deer-hair work and other applications.

On-stream, use the hook from another fly to clear a blocked eye.

Cauterizing tool

LET THEM BREATHE

Air-out fly boxes after each trip to keep your flies from rusting or molding. Do this regardless of whether you took a dunk—water can seep into your boxes from rain or wading too deep.

STEAM SOLUTION

To rejuvenate matted hackles on your dry flies or crinkly bucktails on your Clousers, place the flies in a colander over a steaming teapot. Don't put the flies in the main blast of steam though. You can also hold individual flies over steam with forceps.

FREEING SNAGS

Relax. The best thing to do when you snag your fly is to not make it worse. Don't pull hard on the fly or violently shake your rod. Take a second to compose yourself before resorting to one of the alternatives that follow. When you retrieve your fly from a snag, check your leader and tippet for abrasion and check the hook point to make sure the hook is still sharp.

Snags on the Bottom
From your position, strip out a generous amount of line and let it float downstream of the snag. Sometimes line tension on the water pulls the snag free.

Move downstream or upstream of the snag and pull gently. Sometimes a different angle helps.

Wade out to the snag, and try to free the fly with your feet.

Snags on Logs and Rocks
Roll cast your line to free a snag. Move so that you can roll cast from different angles. If this fails, wade out and get it.

Snags in Trees
Slowly creep the fly out of the bushes or leaves. Many times it will come free.

If it is stuck, try having a partner pull the limb down to free the snag, or use a long stick to pull the limb down.

Roll cast to free snag

If you snag your fly on a limb, take all the line and tippet into your rod and gently unsnag it with your rod tip. Be careful not to force the rod tip.

Last resort: Point the rod tip at the snag and pull on the fly line until the fly breaks off. When you pull, make sure your fly rod tip is absolutely straight.

REMOVING FISH HOOKS

Debarb all hooks at the vise or before you leave for a trip to avoid any nasty in-the-field hook-removal surgery. A hook with its barb pinched all the way down is a snap to remove. If you or your partner forgets to debarb the hook, and it somehow finds its way into your flesh, here's how some experts recommend removing it. If a hook is embedded near or in your eye, cover it with a loose dressing and get to the hospital immediately.

Back Up and Push
Push down on the hook shank to help disengage the barb from the skin. Back the hook out.

The Yank
Numb the wound with ice, if you have any. Loop 0X tippet material around the hook bend, then wrap both ends of the monofilament around your hand several times so it doesn't slip when you pull. Have the victim push down on the flesh above the hook barb and hold the hook eye down at the same time to ensure the hook comes out at the right angle. Yank the tippet or leader material with a single strong stroke and the hook usually comes free.

Back up and push

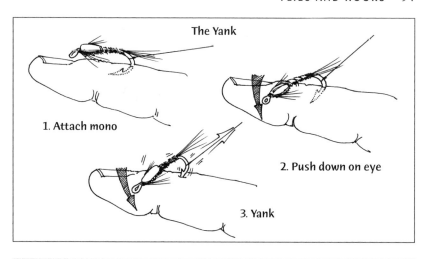

The Yank

1. Attach mono

2. Push down on eye

3. Yank

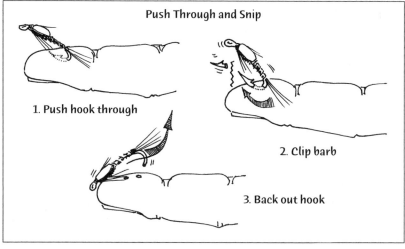

Push Through and Snip

1. Push hook through

2. Clip barb

3. Back out hook

Sneak attack variation: Tell them that you'll pull on a count of three and have them start counting. After "one," yank the tippet or leader material while applying pressure to the shank. Don't be timid when you pull—pretend you are starting a lawn mower. It's possible to merely tug the hook and cause pain but impossible to free the hook too quickly.

Push Through and Snip

The last resort, and most drastic method, is to push the hook through and cut the shank with pliers or push down the barb if you can. Then, back the hook out.

7

Leaders, Tippets, and Knots

LEADERS AND TIPPETS

PERFECT CURVES

When dry-fly fishing, constantly adjust your tippet based on the fly you are using. If your leader lands straight, add tippet or reduce its diameter; if it lands in a pile, take away tippet or increase diameter.

Ideally, the leader should land with just enough S curves to prevent drag, but allow you to set the hook quickly.

THREAD IT

So you always can find the tip of your leader, thread it through the holes in the side of your reel after you reel up. This also prevents underwrapping the line on the reel, where forward portions of the fly line are under rear portions of the fly line—a serious problem if you fish for saltwater fish or trout that can get into your backing, and a common problem if you aren't careful about keeping the tippet end free.

Perfect curves

DON'T BITE TIPPETS

Not only does biting tippets wear grooves in your teeth, but you can get *Giardia* and other nasties from a little contact with contaminated water.

GET IT STRAIGHT

Before fishing, stretch your leader by running your hands along it. Stroke the butt repeatedly until it is straight, applying as much pressure as you can, and heat from friction will straighten the leader. Stretching your leader with your hands is also a good way to check for wind knots and abrasions, which can weaken your leader. Store-bought leader straighteners (generally two rubber pads covered with fabric or leather) are unnecessary and can generate too much heat that can weaken monofilament nylon tippets.

FLEXIBLE WEIGHT

For many years, anglers advocated for what Montana guide Neale Streeks calls "Axis" leaders—stiff

Exploding Leaders

Store-bought leaders seem to explode when you try to unwrap them. Hold open the coils with your fingers while you unwrap the heavy (butt) end four or five times.

German monofilament butts (Mason or Maxima) and supple Japanese tippet sections. But, many good casters think that overly stiff leader butts impede the turnover of your leader, actually opening up the loop, and that the best leader butts are supple and match both the diameter and stiffness of the fly line.

Be a Good Neighbor

Always pick up discarded fishing line when you see it on-stream. It kills birds.

SHORT AND SIMPLE

When fishing sinking lines, a single piece of leader material, or a two-part leader, is all that you need. Also, use a short leader, from 2 to 4 feet (depending on water clarity), with sinking lines. It's easier to cast and sinks the fly deeper.

REPLACE OLD TIPPET

Don't be a cheapskate and horde nylon monofilament tippet (3X to 8X) over the years. Monofilament degrades and becomes weaker when exposed to moisture and ultraviolet light. Save yourself the heartache of a lost fish and buy new tippets each year. (Fluorocarbon degrades much more slowly.)

INDICATOR TRICK

The length of leader between your strike indicator and last fly is often too long to attach your fly to the hook keeper. When walking from one spot to another, wrap the leader behind your reel seat, back up the rod shaft, and hook the fly on a guide, then wind the reel to tighten the line and secure the leader and flies while you are walking.

LENGTHEN TIPPET

For tough trout, lengthen tippet before decreasing diameter. That way you'll be sure to use the heaviest tippet possible, which you should always do to land fish quickly.

THE RULE OF 11

Subtract the X number from 11 to find the material's diameter in thousandths of an inch. 4X equals .007", 6X equals .005", and so on.

Indicator trick

HARVEY'S SLACK-LINE LEADER

George Harvey's dry-fly leader, coupled with the slack-line cast, is a deadly combination. Over the years, Harvey has modified his leader design, changing from a stiff to supple butt. Lefty Kreh and others point out that the best leader butts for casting should have flexible weight. The old-school approach of fishing a stiff butt like Maxima or Mason hard nylon doesn't turn over as well as a supple leader material that matches the fly line's diameter and stiffness. The Harvey leader has two parts: the basic leader and the tippet section.

Basic Leader
(Stays constant no matter what tippet size you are building your leader for.)

18 inches of .015-inch diameter,
18 inches of .013-inch diameter,
18 inches of .011-inch diameter, and
18 inches of .009-inch diameter.

Tippet Section
(for a 11' 6" 5X leader)

15 inches of 3X, 15 inches of 4X,
36 inches of 5X.
Note: A shorter leader tapering to 4X
can be made by adding 15 inches of 3X
and 36 inches of 4X.

Clouser's Quick-Turnover Bass Leader

Bob Clouser

These two basic leader formulas build 7-foot leaders to which you can attach from 2 to 4 feet of tippet, giving you a leader that ranges from 9 to 11 feet. They are designed to cast heavy and wind-resistant patterns. Tie loops at the end of each leader for attaching tippets and a loop on the butt end for attaching to a whipped loop on a fly line.

Rod weights, 6 through 8 (for tippets 6- to 10-pound-test)
36 inches of 40-pound-test (.024-inch diameter)
18 inches of 30-pound-test (.022-inch diameter)
10 inches of 25-pound-test (.020-inch diameter)
10 inches of 20-pound-test (.017-inch diameter)
10 inches of 12-pound-test (.013-inch diameter)

Rod weights 8 and 9 (for tippets 6- to 12-pound-test)
36 inches of 50-pound-test (.028-inch diameter)
18 inches of 40-pound-test (.024-inch diameter)
10 inches of 30-pound-test (.022-inch diameter)
10 inches of 20-pound-test (.017-inch diameter)
10 inches of 12-pound-test (.013-inch diameter)

IN THE LOOP

Rig your entire system—backing to fly line, fly line to leader butt, and leader to tippet—with loops for quick changing.

Make the loops in your backing and fly line large enough to pass the reel through for quick changing of your fly lines.

Tie a loop at the end of your leader and attach your tippet loop to loop to save time on-stream and keep from using up your leader by tying knots. Pretie loops in your tippets and carry those in a wallet to avoid carrying tippet spools.

Tie on some flies ahead of time (especially small flies) and loop to loop them to your leader—this works well when fish continue to feed long after you can see. Store these in your boxes, or wrap them up and keep them in small envelopes or film canisters.

Convert a floating line into an instant sink tip by carrying assorted lengths of LC-13 or Rio's T-14 with loops on both ends. Whip loops into the ends or use braided monofilament loops (see "Homemade Braided Loops," page 114) on 6-inch, 1-foot, 3-foot, or 6-foot sections, depending on the water that you fish. Loop sections together for more weight.

Loop-to-loop rigging

KNOTS

KNOT SENSE

Learn all your knots at home, not on the water, and learn to tie a few knots well rather than a lot of knots poorly.

HEAD-TO-HEAD

Attach one knot to a streamer hook and another knot to another hook on about 12 to 16 inches of tippet. Test the knots against each other with both a slow pull and a quick jerk. This will give you confidence in your knots and help you choose the knots you use more wisely. Wear eye protection.

Keep It Square

Two loops joined correctly form a square knot, not a girth hitch. If your connection isn't forming a square knot, you can manipulate the line with your hands so that it seats properly— you don't have to pass one particular end through the other.

PRACTICE MAKES PERFECT

Practice with rope or old fly line. Buy a good fishing knot book such as *Fishing Knots* by Lefty Kreh (Stackpole, 2007), and a good general knot book such as *Chapman's Nautical Knots,* and practice, practice, practice. Learn how to tie off a boat on a cleat, how to tie a clove hitch (once for horses, now a good, quick knot for everything from tying yarn onto a leader or tethering a dog leash to a post), and how to lash down a canoe on top of a car. These knots will come in handy one day.

TEST THEM

Test your knot before fishing it. Once you tie a knot, test it with a smooth pull. Even proficient anglers sometimes make mistakes, and it's better to know sooner that your knot is going to fail than later when you have a fish on the line.

Knots that work well in monofilament don't necessarily perform as well in fluorocarbon. Many find that the improved clinch, for instance, is weaker in fluorocarbon than the regular clinch knot.

QUICK CLINCH

Tie a clinch knot around your finger first and slip it over the bend of a fly for a quick way to rig a dry-and-dropper that doesn't mash the tails of your dry fly. This is perfect for small flies.

Step 1. Make a small loop in one end of the tippet and put two fingers inside the loop.

Step 2. Twist the loop six times with your two fingers, holding the tag end with your other hand.

Step 3. Pass the tag end through the loop.

Step 4. For an improved clinch, pass it through the second loop created by the tag and standing line.

Step 5. Snug up the knot. Put the loop around the bend of the hook you are using for an indicator fly and tighten.

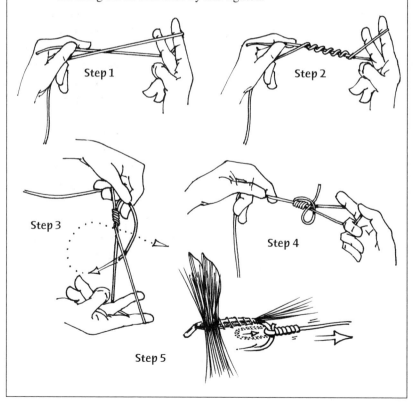

USE THE FORCE(PS)

Use your hemostats to tie some common (and improved) fishing knots.

Forceps Clinch
Step 1. Pass the line through the hook eye and double it back 5 inches.
Step 2. Stick the forceps through the loop and twist five times.
Step 3. Grasp the tag end with your forceps.
Step 4. Pull it through and snug up the knot.

   Note: You can also make this knot without forceps and use your pointer finger to twist the tippet. Stick your thumb through the hole, grab the tag end, and pull it through.

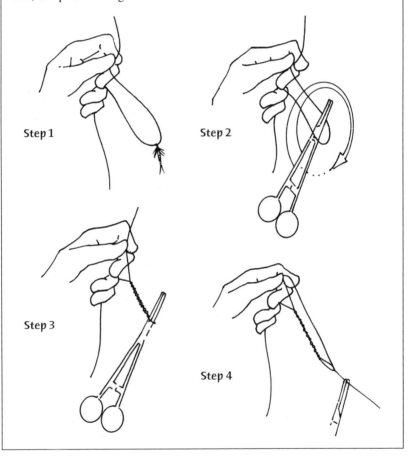

Step 1

Step 2

Step 3

Step 4

GET A GRIP

Knots tied with heavy tippets are hard to seat properly. When tying knots in heavier pound-test leader material, seat the knot with a pair of pliers, and stick the fly in a piece of wood or put the hook bend around something secure like a boat rail and pull tight.

IMPROVED BLOOD KNOT

The more dissimilar the tippet sizes, the more difficult they are to connect. If rebuilding a leader, consider adding short lengths of tippet to build a better transition. If you have to connect dissimilar tippet sizes (2X to 5X, for example), the improved blood knot provides a good, strong connection.

Step 1. Double over the thinner diameter tippet. Make sure that you have 4 to 6 inches to work with.

Step 2. Tie a regular blood knot and trim the tag ends.

Lube Tube

Carry lip balm with you to lube knots. You can put it on your lips and then lube the knot with your lips. That way you won't sunburn your lips and your knots will close easily and smoothly. This works especially well for tying knots in heavier tippets, which are difficult to seat properly.

DON'T MIX MATERIALS

Avoid attaching light monofilament tippet to fluorocarbon nylon, and vice versa. Fluorocarbon is harder than monofilament and can cut into it, weakening the knot.

Improved blood knot

Step 1

Step 2

Use loop knot
for more action

GETTING ACTION

The knot you use to attach tippet to
fly can affect the fly's action: Use a
loop knot to increase the movement
in a fly—even on surface patterns,
such as poppers.

CLINCH KNOT BASICS

*Even though it's not the strongest
knot, many use it anyway—probably
because it's one of the easiest to
remember and tie. Here are a few
things you should know.*

The regular old clinch knot is
stronger than the improved clinch in
fluorocarbon.

If you use a clinch to connect tippet to the bend of a fly for a dropper, tie the knot around your finger
and slip the loop over the bend of
the fly and tighten.

For tippets 8X to 6-pound-test,
use five turns; for tippets 8- to 12-
pound-test, use four turns, and for
tippets heavier than 12-pound, use
another knot.

Gently pull all slack in the spirals
around the standing line by pulling
on the tag end before you cinch the
knot tight.

After lubricating the knot, pull
firmly and smoothly.

Twist It

Instead of wrapping the tag
end around the standing end,
you can hold both ends and
twist the fly. This works especially well with larger flies—dry
flies or wets.

8

Fly Lines and Backing

FLY LINES

CLEANING FLY LINES

If your fly-line tip sinks, chances are your line is dirty. (Another cause of a sinking line tip is a leader butt that may be too heavy.) Other symptoms of a line in need of a good scrubbing are a visibly dirty line, a line that doesn't shoot well, or a line that makes a rattling, scratchy sound as it shoots through the guides.

Not all fly lines are made the same. Some have additives to the coating that help them float and remain supple, while some have internal lubricants. Follow the line manufacturer's recommendations for cleaning.

The best way to clean a line is with soap, not detergent. If the product says "soap" on the label, it's soap. If it doesn't say "soap," don't chance it. Mild soaps such as Ivory hand soap or Woolite are popular choices.

Strip line from the reel in large coils (that land on top of each other) into a bucket, your tub, or sink of warm water with a drop or two of soap.

Clean a dirty line with soap

Do not put in too much soap or you will have trouble getting your line free of the soap, which leaves a film on your line if you don't get it off completely.

Soak the line for about 15 minutes to loosen grit and grime. Scrub the line with a damp cloth or sponge.

Drain the soapy water and fill the sink with clean water. Rinse the sponge or cloth repeatedly to remove all excess soap and dirt.

If you plan on dressing your line, strip the line through a dry cloth onto a clean surface. Apply your dressing on a clean rag and pull the line through it as you reel in.

A line winder makes quick work of cleaning and dressing your fly lines, especially if you store them off the reel. Collapsible ones are great for traveling.

If your Rio or Scientific Anglers' line is really dirty, use one of the mildly abrasive cleaning pads sold by those manufacturers. Rubbing the line with the abrasive pad removes the outer layer of the line coating, releasing more internal lubricants. Wet the pad for the best results, and use the scratchy side, not the sponge side. But don't use these on lines that are coated with lubricants—only use them on lines with internal plasticizers. Check your line manufacturer's instructions.

Line cleaning pad

Practice casting on a lawn and not on dirt or asphalt. If possible, use older lines for these sessions.

Store lines in cool places out of the sun. Don't leave your reel in a hot car for a long time.

Wash Your Hands

Wash your hands carefully after fueling up, or applying bug repellant or suntan lotion. Some suntan lotions, insect repellants, fly floatants, and fuel damage the coating.

TWIST AND SHOUT: REMOVING LINE TWIST

Lines twist over time through improper casting or loading them improperly onto the spool. Line twist becomes pesky if you make a lot of Belgian casts—that handy cast for weighted flies and sinking lines—and twist your wrist. Each cast puts part of a twist in the line. To easily remove the twists, take off the fly, and troll the entire line behind a boat or let the line hang in a river's currents.

Line manufacturer Rio Products recommends removing twists in harder coatings, such as for saltwater lines, by doing the following: Make a long cast. Take the rod loosely at the stripping guide and your other hand on the butt. Quickly rotate the rod, letting the reel flip around (counterclockwise for most right-handed casters) ten to fifteen times, then shake out the line. If this adds more twists, go the other way.

REPAIRING FLY LINES

Fly lines take a lot of abuse—we step on them, run them across rocks, catch them in props. Here's how to salvage a damaged line.

Coat minor nicks with multiple, light applications of a flexible glue such as Goop, Aquaseal, or Pliobond. Thin each of these glues with a thinning product so that they go on light. Once one coating dries, apply another coat until you've built up several layers and the coating is smooth.

If the line is cut to the core, and the gash is a few millimeters or more long, inspect the core. If the core looks okay, wrap tying thread over the cut and then coat in the manner described above.

Recycle Lines Beyond Repair

Old floating fly lines make great strike indicators; lanyards for sunglasses, yard tools, or spare keys; or practice "rope" for knot-tying sessions. Reuse the running line of your floating lines for shooting heads. Make custom sink tips with your old sinking lines.

If you suspect a damaged core, cut out the damaged section and splice the lines together with braided monofilament backing material (see "Joining Lines," page 116).

GET THE KINKS OUT

Improve your distance and accuracy by regularly stretching your fly line before fishing or casting practice.

Wrap the line around a tree, fence post, trailer hitch, or similar object and pull on both ends. Try to find a smooth object that doesn't abrade your line.

Have a partner hold the middle of the line while you pull on both ends, or have them hold one end of a portion of the line that you will be casting—most anglers don't cast farther than 60 feet for trout.

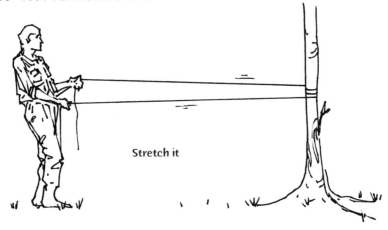

Stretch it

In a boat where space is tight, pull two arm lengths of line off the reel, put it under your foot, and pull up on both ends. Strip more line off the reel and repeat until you've stretched the length of line you will cast.

ORGANIZING LINES
Band-It
If you don't store a line on the spool it came on, you can keep it in a managed coil with twist ties, pipe cleaners cut in half, or rubber bands. Wrap the rubber band around the coil, and pass one end through the larger loop, cinching tight. The rubber band will stay in place. Two opposing places on the loop are good, three evenly spaced spots are best. Velcro strips sold in garden and hardware stores also work well to corral line.

Mark Your Line

Mark the fly line weight with permanent marker. Anglers like Lefty Kreh use long dashes for a five and shorter dashes for one, so a long dash followed by a short dash is the symbol for a 6-weight. Also mark the back end so you can identify your line when you store it on a spool.

▬ =5

AMERICAN FISHING TACKLE MANUFACTURERS ASSOCIATION FLY LINE STANDARDS

Line Size	Weight of First 30 feet (grains)	Acceptable Weight Range
1	60	54–66
2	80	74–86
3	100	94–106
4	120	114–126
5	140	134–146
6	160	152–168
7	185	177–193
8	210	202–218
9	240	230–250
10	280	270–290
11	330	318–342
12	380	368–392

Keep a copy of the AFTMA line grain chart handy. This will help you match shooting heads and unlabelled floating lines to your rods.

Printed Labels

Make your own line labels with your computer. John Ryzanych of Softex suggests printing out a description of the line in the smallest font that you can see. Cut the paper with a straightedge and a razor, and coat it onto your fly line with Softex or other similar flexible glue.

Weigh Them

To identify unmarked lines, weigh them on a line scale (from Umpqua) or a grain scale, because fly-line weights are measured in grains: 16 ounces (1 pound) equals 7,000 grains.

SHOOTING HEADS

Because you only aerialize 20 to 30 feet of a shooting head, you need to make some adjustments when picking the right line to load your rod.

Upline as much as two weights for fast-action rods—that's about 270–290 grains for an 8-weight.

Many experienced striper, steelhead, and salmon fishermen use lead core for most of their shooting heads. Attach loops to the ends (see braided loops) for quick changing. The best lengths for smooth-casting lead-core shooting heads are 27 to 30 feet.

WHIPPED LOOP

Whip-finish a loop in the end of your fly line (if it doesn't already have a loop) to make connecting leaders fast and easy.

Step 1

Step 2

Step 3

Step 1. Increase thread tension on your bobbin by wrapping the thread three to four times around one leg. 6/0 thread is good for most applications. Place the line on a flat, hard surface, and trim off about ½ inch of the line with a razorblade to form a taper (optional). Fold the tip of the line over to form a loop, leaving at least 1 inch of doubled line to wrap your thread over.

Step 2. Hold the end of the thread tight against the loop with your left hand, and twirl the bobbin around the doubled-over ends as tightly as possible, covering the transition area thoroughly.

Step 3. If you don't know how to hand whip-finish, wrap over a loop of monofilament, or dental floss threader, a dozen times.

Step 4

Step 5

Step 6

Step 4. Break off the thread and pass it through the monofilament loop.
Step 5. Pull the thread under the wraps, forming the whip-finish.
Step 6. Coat with Softex or Zap-A-Gap.

If you need a loop in the field and you don't have a bobbin, form a loop in your fly line with two nail knots tied with monofilament.

Whipped-loop variation. Instead of doubling back the fly line, strip some coating from the front portion of the fly line by soaking it in nail-polish remover for 20 seconds or so, and then, holding the core against the fly line, whip-finish up to the fly line, forming the loop.

WHITLOCK'S ZAP-A-GAP LOOP

This handy loop isn't as bulky as a whipped loop.

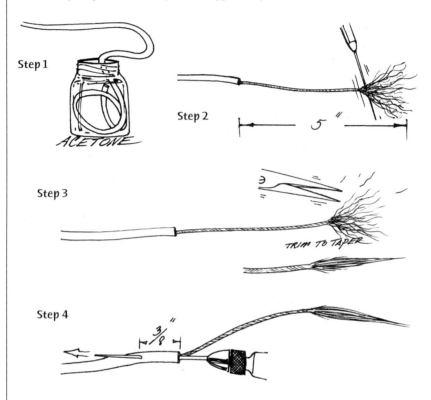

Step 1. Soak 5 to 6 inches of the fly-line tip in nail-polish remover (that contains acetone). Remove the line and strip the coating with your fingernails.

Step 2. Fray the ends of the braided core with a needle, and brush out the individual strands.

Step 3. Thin half of the fibers so that you can thread them through a needle when wet.

Step 4. Insert a dulled #8 or #9 needle into the core where the exposed core meets the fly line. Push the needle into the fly line ³⁄₈ inch and ¹⁄₂ inch out the other side of the fly line.

Step 5. Pass a needle threader through the needle eye, wet the core filaments, and pass them through the threader.

Step 6. Pull the threader through the eye of the needle. Use a pin vise or pliers to pull the needle and core through the fly line and out.

Step 7. Continue to pull on the core until the braided loop is a little larger than you want it. Apply a bit of Zap-A-Gap at the base of the loop.

Step 8. Pull on the core end a little more to pull the Zap-A-Gap inside the fly line, welding the loop core inside the fly line. Cut the excess braided core flush with the exit hole on the fly line and place a drop of Zap-A-Gap on the hole. Pull hard on the loop and fly line to stretch the core and pull the tip inside the fly line.

WHITLOCK'S ZAP-A-GAP SPLICE

This connection is ideal when you won't be changing your leader too frequently, and if you like to use knotless, tapered leaders. It is perfect for 1- to 4-weight trout lines.

Step 1. Put the tip of the needle in a pin vise and push the needle eye through the center of the fly-line core, through the line about ½ inch, and then out the side of the line. If you don't have a pin vise, you can poke the needle eye through the fly line and pull it out the side of the line with pliers.

Step 2. Thread the tippet portion of the tapered leader through the eye (if you have a hard time getting it to fit, trim it at an angle with a razor) at least 2 inches, and pull on the needle, threading the tippet into the fly line and out the end. Pull on the tippet until about 2 inches of the butt section is remaining on the other side of the line.

Step 3

Step 4

Step 3. Tie an overhand knot in the butt section so that you can get a grip on the butt of the leader. Rough up the leader in front of the fly line with sandpaper until it is opaque. Place a drop of Zap-A-Gap on the roughed-up section and pull on the leader butt sharply, pulling the roughed up portion into the fly line.

Step 4. Trim the leader butt flush, place a drop of Zap-A-Gap on the hole, and pull on the leader so that the leader butt goes inside the fly line.

A variation of this technique that some anglers report success with is to rough up the butt section in front of knot and pull on the leader that is extending out of the fly line until the knot jams up against the fly line. Trim the knot, place a drop of Zap-A-Gap, and pull the fly line and leader to smooth the connection out.

HOMEMADE BRAIDED LOOPS

When installed properly, braided monofilament loops act like Chinese finger traps . . . the harder you pull, the tighter they squeeze the fly line. It's easy to make your own. These loops are best for rigging shooting heads, sinking lines, and for connecting trout lines to backing. These loops aren't the best for attaching to the tip of a floating line used for trout fishing because the braided monofilament holds more water than other connections. For more information, see danblanton.com.

If you don't have a braiding needle (available at fly shops that sell braided line) or a bobbin threader, first make a splicing tool for all your future braided loops. Fold a 12-inch length of high E (.012" diameter) guitar string or fishing wire in half, forming a point at the end. With a haywire twist, attach the loose ends of the wire to a swivel attached to a key chain loop, which will give you something to grip when you are pulling it.

Step 1. Braided monofilament is available in different weights from manufacturers such as Gudebrod and Cortland. Lighter braids (30-pound) are good for smaller lines and thin sinking lines; heavier braids (50-pound) for LC-13 or fat saltwater or Spey lines. Pull off a length of braided monofilament. If you want a large loop, you need more; short loops require less. Insert a needle or bobbin threader into the braided monofilament and run it through the line about 1½ to 2 inches and then out the side of the line. Where you insert the needle determines how much of the finger trap that you'll have to thread on your line or shooting head when the loop is done.

Step 1

Step 2

Step 3

Step 4

Step 2. Insert the end of the braided monofilament into the needle opening—a short section. Trim it with scissors so that no more than ⅛ inch sticks out.

Step 3. Gently pull the end completely through and back out of the braid's core, massaging the braided core while you do this to help it through. Continue to pull the long end through the core until it is properly sized. Lefty Kreh suggests putting a small dowel (or pencil) in the loop to prevent pulling it through.

Step 4. Once you have the loop size you desire, trim the tag end sticking out from the side of the braided monofilament core so that it is no more than 1½ inches long. Re-insert the needle through the braided line.

Step 5. Run the tag through the braided line again to form a double catch, less than ¼ inch.

Step 6. Put your hand or finger in the loop and stretch everything, smoothing it out, then cut off the shorter tag remaining flush with the braid's wall. Pull on the loop and standing length, and the tag you just cut off will pull up inside the braid's core. Smooth the entire splice with your fingers.

Step 7. Insert the end of the fly line, shooting head (leader or shooting line end), or shooting line into the braided monofilament and inchworm it until it enters the core of the buried tag ⅛ inch.

Step 8. Tie a nail knot just above where the line enters the braid with 10- to 12-pound-test monofilament or tying thread. Trim the tag ends of the braid close to the nail knot. Coat the nail knot and the area where the end of the line enters the tag core with flexible cement such as Pliobond.

Step 5

Step 6

Step 7

Step 8

CAUCCI'S KRAZY GLUE SPLICE

Al Caucci teaches this method to his students at his schools on the West Branch of the Delaware River near Hancock, New York.

Step 1. Soak ⅜ inch of the end of the fly line in fingernail polish (acetone) for about 20 seconds before stripping the fly line coating with your fingernail.

Step 2. Enlarge the exposed core with a large pin or bodkin. Push the leader butt into the exposed core and put a drop of Krazy Glue (original formula) onto the connection. Wet your thumb and forefinger and roll the connection around.

Step 3. Wipe a second drop on the opposite side of the connection and roll the connection around again to thoroughly penetrate the connection with glue. Do not use too much glue. The braided core holds the leader butt, and the glue holds the core in place.

JOINING LINES

Joining two lines with braided leader material is the easiest way to create shooting heads or to repair a line with a splice.

Step 1. Cut a 6-inch piece of braided monofilament. Inch one end of the line halfway into the braided monofilament.

Step 2. Inch the other end of the line into the braided monofilament until it meets the first line.

Step 3. Whip-finish both of the frayed ends of the braided monofilament with thread and coat with flexible cement or glue.

Garth's GSP Splice

Max Garth

Gel-spun polyethylene (GSP) backing can cut through your fly line like butter and it does not hold a knot well. The best method to attach GSP backing to fly line is with a coaxial GSP splice. It takes some time, but the results are worth the effort.

Step 1. Use a 6-inch doll needle to insert a loop of monofilament into the braided monofilament where you want the splice.

Step 2. Push the GSP through the hollow braided monofilament using the doll needle.

Step 3. Tease out the end of the braided monofilament ¼ inch. Put the line, GSP, and braided monofilament into the monofilament loop, making sure that the monofilament loop is on the teased-out section of the tag end, and pull it through into the braided monofilament. Teasing out the end makes it a bit easier to get the braided monofilament back into itself.

Step 4. Pull the braided monofilament through the splice section, trim the end so it's square (no funny ends), and pull the end back into the splice.

Step 5. Apply one drop of LocTite 406 CA glue to the middle of the spliced section and let it cure for about an hour. Test it for security. Loctite 406 saturates the GSP, and when cured holds it solidly in place.

BACKING

Backing's primary purpose on trout reels is to increase the circumference of your fly reel's arbor so you can reel in line with maximum efficiency and prevent tight coils in your lines. On reels for larger game, backing provides insurance against fish that make long runs. Backing comes in two types: Dacron and GSP (gel-spun polyethylene).

Inspect your backing for damage a few times a year.

Clean all the salt from your backing and let the reel dry in the open for several days if a fish runs into your backing in salt water, or you dunk your reel in salt water.

Cut some running line from your fly line to increase the backing capacity of your reel. Many fly lines are over 100 feet long—much longer than what most of us can cast effectively.

Bright orange or yellow backing helps you track what your line is doing when you are fighting a fish that has taken out all of your fly line.

Tie a big loop into your backing so that you can quickly change lines with a loop-to-loop connection.

INSTALLING BACKING
Ask a Pro
The best way to install backing is with a backing winder, available at most fly shops and sporting-goods stores. Buy your backing from someone who will install it for you.

DIY Tips
If you are going to install backing on the spool yourself, it's critical that you wind it tightly and evenly. Experiment to find what method works best for you.

Put the backing spool in a small box (so it doesn't jump and skitter all over the place) and wind it through a big, closed book such as a dictionary.

You can also try sticking a pencil or dowel through the hole in the floor and step on both ends of the pencil or dowel with bare feet (it helps to place the spool on a plastic mat or something else to prevent scuffing the floor) to keep tension on the spool.

Another alternative is to first wind the backing onto a reel, adjust that reel with approximately 3 pounds of drag, and then wind your backing on your primary reel, using the secondary reel's tension.

Be sure to wind the backing back and forth from one side of the spool to the other so the backing doesn't pile up on one side and then fall over on itself.

With GSP backing, use a finger guard or glove to prevent cutting your hands.

SIMPLIFIED GSP SPLICE

Follow the directions for the braided loop, but first run your GSP through the braided monofilament. Thread the GSP through your braided running line with a splicing needle (to make one, see Braided Loops, page 114) and follow the directions for a braided loop, bypassing the double-catch step. Add a drop of Loctite 406.

GSP CAT'S PAW

Tie a Bimini twist in the GSP backing and loop to a loop on the fly line with a cat's paw, a series of loops formed by repeatedly (three or four times) placing the reel with GSP through the fly-line loop, giving several places of grip. One of the loops needs to be large enough to pass the reel or the coiled line through.

9

Rods, Reels, and Other Equipment

RODS

FREEING STUCK FERRULES

Get a Grip
Carry rubber jar openers in your gear bag to help get a grip on a rod when you break it down; rubber kitchen gloves and rubber shelf liners cut to size also work.

Bend a Little
For a stubborn rod that won't come apart, grip the rod joint behind your knees and grasp the rod with each hand on the outside of each knee. Slowly spread your knees apart.

Chill
Try chilling the ferrules (remember cold contracts things; heat swells). If you are near water, stick the rod in the stream for five minutes. During the summer (when this usually happens), trout rivers should be cool enough to contract the female end. Use cold running water or ice (with tin foil, build a "dam" around the ferrule and load it with ice for 20 minutes or more) or used crushed ice in a Ziploc bag. Then, with your left hand and a grip aid (see above) rotate one way, and with your right hand rotate the other way while pulling the sections apart. Some anglers have had good luck by blasting the ferrules with canned air to chill them.

Wax the male ferrule to prevent ferrules from sticking and to ensure you have a tight joint while casting and fighting fish.

LAST OUT, FIRST IN

When beginning a trip, get all your gear ready and then take out your rod; when you return, put your rod away first.

Don't lean your rod against the side or put it on top of your vehicle. Put it on your hood so that you see it before you drive away.

ASSEMBLING RODS

Inspect ferrules for grit and clean and wax if necessary. Sand in the female end can damage the male end or result in a stuck ferrule. Blow into the open ferrules before putting the rod together.

Insert the male into the female ferrule so that the guides are at right angles to one another. Gently but firmly twist them into place, and

Breaking and Entering

More fly rods are broken by screen doors and car windows than from fighting fish. Don't take assembled rods indoors and don't stick them out of your car window if you have power windows—even if you think you are smarter than the next guy.

check alignment by sighting down the guides. Some rods have dots and other markers to indicate that the sections are straight.

Never hold onto the snake guides when twisting your rod together or apart. They are weak and can break easily.

Continue with the other sections. For a four-piece rod, do the two bottom pieces, the two top pieces, and then put the two sections together.

Don't pull line from your reel by drawing the line up through the guides and then back down toward your reel. Always pull the line directly from the reel.

Rig your rod on-stream. You can watch the water for clues while you rig up, and you arrive at the stream receptive to ideas. If you tie on your flies in the parking lot, you tend to start casting as soon as you get to the water, but the best anglers take their time and look for clues first.

Loop the fly line and pass the looped line through the guides when you are stringing a rod. Once you pull the looped line out of the tip guide, there's no need to continue pulling everything through—just cast the rod a few times and the line and leader will come out.

Stringing Up in Tight Quarters

Assemble a rod in a boat (or elsewhere where space is tight) by first stringing the bottom half of the rod, then the next half—before you put the pieces together.

ROD CARE

Check your ferrules often while you are fishing and tighten them if they come loose.

Small scratches on the insides of your guides can damage the line. Several times a year inspect the rod rings with a magnifying glass or slip a wad of cotton through them. Small scratches will hold some cotton.

Rinse your rod with fresh water and dry it with a soft cloth before putting it back into its sock. Don't put your rod away wet. If you must, wash and dry the sock thoroughly as soon as possible to prevent mold.

To clean a grimy rod, wash it with lukewarm soapy water and a soft sponge. Scrub the dirt from the guides and reel seat with a toothbrush.

TUBE TIPS

When you slide your rod into the tube (after it's in the sock), make a circle with your thumb and forefinger, and slide the sock through it into the tube to prevent banging your guides against the lip of the tube, which is one of the most common ways they are damaged.

Make your own rod tubes out of PVC pipe.

Leave caps off the tubes to prevent mold and mildew if you store your rods in a humid environment such as some basements.

Don't stow a rod in its tube for long periods of time. This can trap humidity, which corrodes guide rings and other problems. Instead, hang it in its sock on a clothes hanger in your closet. If you have to store it in the tube, take the cap off; or, if there's room, slip a package of silica crystals in the closed tube. This is where large tubes designed to accommodate several rods come in handy. Silica packets—available in the laundry section of most grocery stores—are great anywhere you don't want mold: such as in camera cases or Rubbermaid containers where you store your gear over the winter.

TRAVELING WITH RODS

If you assemble your rod at the car, make sure you also pass the line through it and tie on a fly before a long walk in the woods. The line will keep your rod together. Many rod sections have been lost this way and you cannot use your repair warranty on a rod's missing pieces.

Before a walk through a lot of brush, leave the rod in its sock and assemble it on-stream.

Go butt first with the tip of the rod angled behind you to keep out of tangles when walking through the woods.

Windshield wipers can hold your rod on your windshield while you travel short distances. Place the rod tip going back over the car and don't use your wipers.

Carry rod tubes and rods easily by taking a tip from Lefty Kreh. He attaches a short length of strap material to the tube with two large stainless-steel adjustable clamps for a convenient handle.

Larger cases that accommodate up to four rods in their sleeves save space, keep your rods organized, and are easier to carry.

Write your name, phone number, and address on your rod tube or tape a business card to the tube. While you're at it, write your contact information on your fly boxes. That way the person who finds it knows who it belongs to.

Bamboo Rods

Jerry Kustich

Over the past five years there has been a Gold Rush–style enthusiasm for quality old and new rods by those who are now discovering the joy of fishing with a natural material that perfectly connects them to the water running through their lives. Whether handed down from a father or grandfather, a bamboo rod connects you to the past.

For most bamboo craftsmen, the foremost question often asked is about the durability of bamboo rod, especially considering the investment required to purchase a quality rod these days. Although a cane rod tip won't be anymore successful stopping a car door than its graphite counterpart, in unison all bamboo artisans will state that bamboo is much more durable. Some may even throw a blank on the floor, and step all over the section just to prove the point. That said, a bamboo rod takes a bit more TLC in terms of maintenance, if only to protect and preserve the value—particularly as an heirloom to be handed down to future generations to enjoy. What follows are a few tips to consider in caring for a new or old bamboo rod.

Check old rods periodically for seam failure, loose ferrules and guides, or breakdown in the protective finish. Glue and finish materials from the past often break down, so it is important to keep an eye on a classic. This can be done under a bright light, and most irregularities should be obvious. It doesn't hurt to have an expert check the rod out now and then.

Check ferrule fit. One of the most common problems with bamboo is the fit at the ferrule, which can get tighter over time because the metal oxidizes or gathers specks of grime. This problem can be avoided by regularly swabbing the male and female portions of the ferrule with denatured alcohol on a tissue or a Q-tip. This is particularly essential after fishing in the rain or a damp fog, since moisture can enhance the corrosion factor. If alcohol doesn't do it, a light rub with 0000 steel wool can penetrate the film. Beyond that, consult an expert.

Never lubricate a ferrule so it slides together better. Often this leads to gathering more grime and a tighter fit that becomes impossible to pull apart. If you feel the need to use a lubricant, it is time to clean your ferrules instead.

Detach the ferrules each day after use. Keep the rod strung for a long time and the ferrules may lock together.

If the ferrule fit is too loose, get it adjusted by an expert. A short-term fix, however, is to rub paraffin on the male portion to fill the gap and keep the ferrules together. Too much wax over time can lead to a build up and ferrules that stick together too tightly.

Never put a bamboo rod away wet. Wiping a rod down and letting it air dry is the simplest form of maintenance to avoid long-term regrets.

Store bamboo rods in a closet rather than a basement. Dampness can lead to mold, mildew, and other problems that can be easily avoided by storage in a dry setting.

A "set" in a tip of a bamboo rod is a distinct curve in one direction that occurs over time, mostly due to fighting fish. Minimize the risk of putting a set in your rod by occasionally rotating the rod while fighting each fish.

At the end of each season, examine a rod for developing flaws and clean and polish it with any product safe for fine furniture.

Although a bamboo rod is resilient, common sense is the best rule. Lifetime warranties on graphite rods may lead to a more carefree attitude since the rod will be replaced with no questions asked. This policy does not apply to most bamboo rods. However, a bamboo rod will stand the test of time if given the respect that it deserves.

CLEANING GRIPS

Dirty cork grips not only look unsightly, they are slippery. A regular cleaning improves performance.

Scrub with soap and an old toothbrush or similar small brush to cut any grease (Simple Green also works) and then follow up with a scouring cleaner such as Comet or Soft Scrub with Bleach. Some anglers use Wonder Cloth or Mr. Clean's Magic Eraser to clean cork grips.

Sand grips with a fine-grit (200) sandpaper to clean them, but be careful. You can also sand your grip (fine grit) by hand for a custom fit. A lot of grips are too large, especially if you have small hands. But be warned that you might void your warranty.

Grip Repair

Repair missing chunks in your cork grip with wood filler or wood filler mixed with cork dust to the consistency of peanut butter. Slightly overfill hole, let it dry overnight, and sand. You can also fill the hole with a mixture of wine-cork dust and epoxy, and sand.

PURCHASING RODS

Use the same line when you compare rods, because a fly line affects how a rod performs.

When choosing a rod for fishing small flies or small streams, be sure to test how well it loads at distances of around 30 feet or less. Most of your fishing will be at this range, because you won't be able to see the fly any farther than that. The same rod that loads at this short distance will probably have a slower action or at least a softer tip, which is essential for protecting the light tippets necessary for small flies.

Short rods (6 to 7½ feet) are best for tight, brushy streams; long rods better for large rivers, lakes, or drift boats. Most people purchase 8½- or 9-foot rods, but 10-foot rods can give you an advantage in float-tube fishing and steelheading.

A wiggle in the shop won't help when buying a rod. If you can, ask the proprietor to cast the rod first, with several different line weights.

REELS

ROUTINE MAINTENANCE

To prevent sand and grit from working their way into your reel, rest the rod butt and reel on your shoe or other clean surface—instead of putting it directly on the ground—while you are stringing your rod.

Store reels outside of their pouches to prevent trapped moisture.

Prevent corrosion after saltwater use by rinsing your reel immediately with warm fresh water. For additional protection, use an anticorrosive treatment available from many reel manufacturers.

If you spray your reel with a hose, you risk driving salt deeper into the reel. Run it under a faucet and warm water instead.

If your reel has a cork drag, keep the drag tight while you are washing your reel to prevent water from reaching the drag; when you store the reel, loosen the drag.

Clean around reel feet and other hard-to-get areas with a toothbrush.

To add an additional protective layer on your reel, clean it with alcohol and then coat it with a hard car paste wax. Some recommend applying Lemon Pledge to the reel to make water bead up easier.

If you dunk your reel completely in the salt (something you should always avoid), take it apart completely and clean the parts individually. Send high-quality reels back to the manufacturer as soon as possible for a professional cleaning. Saltwater reels with sealed drags can be completely submerged in warm soapy water for a thorough cleaning. Call your reel's manufacturers for their specific instructions.

Salt Spray

Cold water doesn't get rid of salt. Keep hot soapy water in one spray bottle and rinse reels with hot, clean water from another.

Leather or suede reel pouches lined with sheepskin are not good for saltwater use—they trap moisture and can't be washed. Neoprene is better.

Traditionally anglers used a little Neet's Foot Oil on their cork drags once they started to squeak or become rough. Some reel manufacturers (Tibor, for instance) say that Neet's Foot Oil can dry out the cork over time. Instead, they recommend a lubricant with graphite powder. On his website, danblanton.com, Dan Blanton recommends Fluid Film for one-way bearings, races, shafts, and silicone grease with powdered graphite for cork and fiber drags.

Keep the reel in its protective case while on the rod so it doesn't bang against the side of the boat or elsewhere while the boat is running.

DRAGS

If you can pull off line with your dry lips, then the drag is set properly for most species, approximately 12 ounces of pressure. For big fish like tarpon, set your drag at 2 pounds (straight pull) with a scale.

The amount of pressure it takes to pull line off your reel when it is full with line is different than with an empty reel. The drag is heavier with less line, which sometimes can account for lost fish on lighter tippets.

REELING IN LINE

You don't reel the fish in with your reel. You fight with the rod and reel to recover the line.

Wide-arbor spools are popular but if you don't wind on the backing and line carefully, it piles up on one side of the spool and then eventually topples. Narrow spools allow you to recover line evenly, even if you are not paying attention

If you make a living with your hands, invest in an antireverse reel, which has a handle that won't spin when a fish rips off line.

On direct-drive reels, handles that are triangle shape (fat to small) allow your fingers to slip away faster when a fish runs, preventing knuckle busters.

To prevent knuckle busters, hold the end of the reel handle with your three fingers, rather than grip the reel handle with your thumb, pointer, and middle fingers.

Many veteran saltwater anglers advocate learning to wind the reel with your dominant hand. While you may be able to reel with your left for a short period, you won't be able to for 30 minutes or more, which is about how long it would take to fight a tarpon or tuna—if you are really good, or really lucky.

WADERS AND WADING BOOTS

CUFF CONTROL

Prevent pant legs from riding up by tucking each pant cuff in your socks, before pulling on your waders. Velcro straps sold to bicyclists for keeping pant cuffs clean also hold your pant in place and don't wrinkle cuffs like tucking them in does.

BRACE YOURSELF

A back-brace belt sold in many department stores saves your back when wading all day and doubles as a wading belt.

CHEAP INSURANCE

Keep a spare garbage bag in your vest for streamside trash, emergency poncho, or a short-term patch if you get a leak in your waders at the foot or lower leg. Use the bag as an inside liner until you get home.

TAKE A LOAD OFF

If you have space in your car or truck, a folding camp chair is a nice comfort for changing in and out of waders as well as having in case you want to sit and enjoy a post–fishing trip beverage or cigar.

CARE AND CLEANING OF WADERS

Hang breathable waders when you store them. For longer storage times, roll them up. Folding breathable waders weakens the seams and causes leaks.

Stand on a piece of spare carpet or your car floor mat while you change your waders to save wear and tear on your neoprene booties.

Carry a Rubbermaid container in the back of your car for waders and boots, and stand on the lid while you change in and out of your waders so that you don't ruin the neoprene booties. These containers are also great for organizing your fishing gear and store easily on shelves.

Wash breathable waders by hand in the bathtub. Several manufacturers recommend using cold water and powdered detergent. Rinse completely, hang, and air dry. Do not put them in the dryer or dry clean them.

Treat breathable waders with Revivex, Nikwax, or other durable water repellant when the waders are still wet. Once they drip dry, set the treatment with a blow drier (on low or medium heat). Though not recommended by some manufacturers, many anglers have good success applying the waterproofing and putting the waders in the dryer on medium heat for 8 to 10 minutes.

NEW ZEALAND MUDSNAILS

New Zealand Mudsnails (NZMS) are an invasive-species threat to trout streams spread through waders and wading boots. These cleaning instructions also work to stop the spread of other dangerous aquatic hitchhikers such as whirling disease and Didymo.

Sanitize your wading equipment before traveling to new water. Visual inspection is inadequate.

According to experts, the best cleaner for your waders and boots is *undiluted* Commercial Solutions Formula 409 Cleaner Degreaser Disinfectant or "Formula 409 All Purpose Cleaner Antibacterial

Kitchen Lemon Fresh."
Key words to look for are "Disinfectant" or "Antibacterial."

Bleach is no longer recommended for NZMS, though a 5 to 10 percent bleach solution kills other invasive species such as whirling disease, Didymo, and zebra mussels. Grapefruit seed extract, once considered effective for NZMS, has failed several tests.

Remove inner soles before cleaning and rinse them well to remove cleaning agents before use.

Completely immerse your gear in the solution in a dry bag or 5-gallon bucket for approximately 10 minutes, and then rinse in clean water. Don't forget to clean your wading staff.

New Zealand mudsnail

Other Ways to Disinfect Your Gear

Hot-water bath (120 to 130 degrees F) for at least 5 minutes or put them in the dishwasher.

Dry heat. Spray with Commercial Solutions Formula 409 Cleaner Degreaser Disinfectant or other soap/detergent (the soap breaks down the mucus that the snail uses to hold onto wet surfaces) and let waders and boots dry for several hours—all mud must be completely dry. The air must be low humidity and over 84 degrees F for 24 hours or 104 degrees F (or higher) for 2 hours.

Freeze equipment for at least 4 hours, preferably overnight. This is good for winter anglers or if you have a chest freezer. Thaw waders before bending them.

Clean boats, rafts, and trailers of mud, vegetation, and other debris with a pressure washer or commercial car wash before driving into the next watershed.

REPAIRING WADERS

Send waders with leaky seams or booties back to the manufacturer.

For larger tears, use the wader-repair patch and glue included with your waders. Follow manufacturer's instructions.

Find leaks in neoprene booties by filling the bootie with water and marking where it starts to turn dark and leak. Make sure the outside is completely dry before doing this. Patch with Aquaseal.

Repair leaks on-stream with duct tape (good) or ultraviolet-light cure wader-repair products (better). Use duct tape on both sides of the leak. UV-cure product from Loon Outdoors works on dry or wet waders, cures in minutes, and a small tube fits easily in your fishing kit.

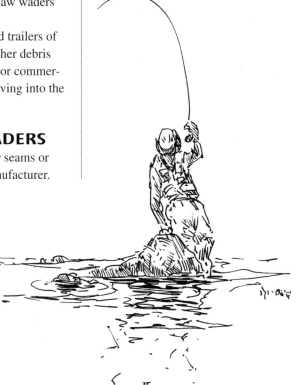

PIN-HOLE LEAKS

Washing your waders and then drying them on low to medium heat often seals small pin-hole leaks. If this doesn't do the trick, you have to find and repair individual leaks.

A dab of Aquaseal is what you usually need to patch small pin-hole leaks—let it dry for at least 6 hours.

Some substitute silicone bathroom caulk or Shoe Goo for Aquaseal.

Once you find the leak, circle it with a waterproof marker on the inside of your waders.

Alcohol

Turn waders inside out. Spray a light application of rubbing alcohol on suspect areas with a spray bottle. Leaks will show as dark gray spots on the outside of the waders.

Bubbles

Put waders in the water, not water in the waders. Some recommend filling waders with water to detect leaks, but a better way that doesn't stress the seams of your waders is to inflate your waders in a tub of water and look for tiny bubbles, which signal leaks. With the waders in the water, bunch the top of your waders around a vacuum (that blows air), leaf blower (on low), or hair dryer (on low heat) until they are inflated, and examine each section in the water.

Instead of immersing them in water, you can also try having a partner spray the waders with a sprayer bottle of soapy water or paint soapy water onto the inflated waders. A leak will be easiest to spot if you avoid creating bubbles when brushing the mixture on the waders.

Rinse the waders with clear water and allow them to dry. Patch with Aquaseal.

Flashlight

In a dark room, slide a flashlight around against the inside of the waders and look for light shining through. Pinch the potential leak, turn your waders inside out, and circle it with marking pen.

WADING BOOT CARE AND COMFORT

Tighten the laces on your wading boot after you've been in the water for awhile. They may loosen over time, and your boots should be snug for the most support. Carry an extra shoelace in case you break one on your wading boots. Some rot over time.

Don't leave boots outside or in the car in cold weather—they can freeze. If you must leave them outside, thaw them in the water before putting them on, or put them away with the tongues as far open as you can so that if they freeze, they at least freeze open.

Some boots shrink and stiffen after they've been in storage. It's much easier to get your feet in them if you wet them first.

Wear neoprene socks under your wading boots in the summer to wet wade.

Make your own stream cleats by drilling twelve to fifteen sheet-metal screws (#6, $\frac{3}{8}$- to $\frac{1}{2}$-inch long, slotted hex washer head) into your felt soles. You can also use screws to quickly repair felt soles that start to separate from the bottom of your boots.

SOLE PATROL

Pick the right wading shoe sole for the job.

Rubber

Pros. Inexpensive, easy to clean, good for snow.

Cons. Not good for any wading except in sandy or gravelly stream bottoms; tend to have poor support.

Sticky Rubber

Pros. Easy to clean, good for walking in snow, moderate to good gripping on clean rocks; more durable for hiking.

Cons. Expensive. Poor traction on algae-covered rocks.

Keep a Clean Car

Dirty wading boots quickly ruin your vehicle's upholstery. Turn your floor mats around, rubber side up, if wearing boots in the car.

Felt

Pros. Most common, affordable. Good all-around sole for a wide variety of stream bottoms.

Cons. Wears easily when hiking; collects snow, making it hard to walk; hard to clean and may contribute to spread of whirling disease more; slippery on wet grass.

Studs

Pros. The best traction when combined with either a felt or composite (sticky rubber) sole.

Cons. Damages fiberglass-bottom drift boats and can tear inflatable rafts. May damage floors indoors; expensive.

Cleats

Pros. Good for jetties, algae-covered rocks, salmon streams, icy rocks.

Cons. Heavy, hard to walk in. Slippery on dry rocks. Not allowed in fly shops or drift boats. Can chew up fly lines if you step on them.

OTHER EQUIPMENT

FISHING YARNS AND OTHER STRIKE INDICATORS

Simple Slip Knot

For a quick way to attach a yarn indicator to your leader butt, place macramé or other yarn in a slip knot and draw it tight. Apply floatant to a small brush and comb out the fibers. Trim as necessary. This rig kinks your leader, but it is quick.

The Clincher

Tie a small piece of yarn with a clinch knot and 3X to 5X monofilament to your leader. This rig doesn't mess with your leader, so you can quickly modify your dry-fly leader to fish nymphs in a pinch. Tie the yarn onto a knot on your leader, and it stays put better.

Uni-Fied

Place the yarn in between back-to-back Uni knots or in the hole in the middle of a blood knot before you cinch it tight.

Rig the Right-Angle

This setup is equally at home in Western pocketwater, Eastern spring creeks, or Great Lakes steelhead streams. The nymph floats directly under the indicator, allowing for better drifts and giving you a better sense of where the nymph is.

Use a straight piece of stout (2X or so) tippet connected with a clinch knot or Duncan loop to the yarn, which can be made from macramé yarn, Widow's Web, or Glo Bug Yarn treated with floatant. Before the yarn, connect a straight piece of tippet with a clinch or Duncan loop and attach your fly to it. When fishing, mend your line so the indicator floats upstream of the nymph immediately after the indicator hits the water. One of the downsides of this rig is that you are committed to nymphing with it and you have to rerig leaders if you switch to dry flies—or you can carry two rods.

Unified

Rig the right-angle

BAND TOGETHER

Dick Galland recommends using a puffball nymphing rig, based on the right-angle leader system. To form the indicator, Galland uses small orthodontic rubber bands that allow you to easily slide this indicator up and down your leader to adjust depth.

Step 1

Step 3

Step 2

Step 4

Step 1. Form a loop in your leader and pass it through a rubber band spread with forceps.

Step 2. Wrap the loop around one side of the rubber band three or four times. Release the rubber band so that it is tight around the leader, forming a loop.

Step 3. Put the macramé yarn into the loop and cinch up the rubber band so that the loop is tight.

Step 4. Brush out the indicator yarn. Add floatant to the brush and yarn. Trim if necessary.

Improved Slip Knot

Charlie Craven

The yarn indicator is the most sensitive indicator I have found. While commercially made versions are available, I prefer to tie my own from macramé yarn directly into the leader butt. The knot I use is a relatively simple slip knot, but I attach the yarn in a unique manner. Follow the directions closely and try this indicator the next time you're out. It is more buoyant, visible, and sensitive than any other indicator, and while it can be a bit harder to cast than other, more streamlined, indicators, the sensitivity far outweighs any liabilities.

Step 1. Make the slip knot where you want the indicator.

Step 2. Place the yarn clump on the line on the underside of the standing line to the left of the loop. Prepare the yarn clump ahead of time by combing out (a wire dog brush works well) 3 inches of braided polypropylene macramé yarn, working from the center toward the ends.

Step 3. Fold the center of the yarn around the standing line. Keep the clump together in a tidy bunch. Grasp the base of the yarn in your left hand along the standing line to keep it all together. (Fingers aren't depicted in the illustration to clearly show the indicator and leader.)

Step 4. Open the loop up and slide the fingers of your right hand down through the loop. Grasp the base of the yarn tightly while drawing the tippet end down to tighten the loop around its base.

Step 5. Continue to draw the loop down until it is completely cinched around the base of the yarn.

Step 6. Pull tightly on both ends of the standing line to secure the knot. Trim the yarn square across the top. Use larger indicators in fast water or with more weight on the leader. Trim it shorter when in shallow water or when using just a little bit of weight. Apply your favorite paste or liquid floatant to the yarn before you fish.

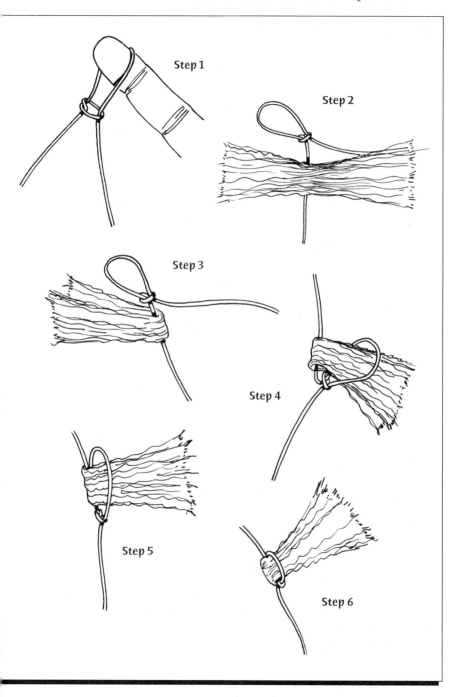

Step 1

Step 2

Step 3

Step 4

Step 5

Step 6

REUSABLE YARN INDICATORS

Make reusable indicators with tying thread and yarn. Use two different colors of yarn for good visibility under a broad range of lighting conditions—like white and black or black and yellow. Attach the indicator 1½ to 2 times the water depth you are fishing. Attach the indicator to the leader by passing the looped leader through the loop in the indicator and over the yarn. Vary indicator size depending on water conditions.

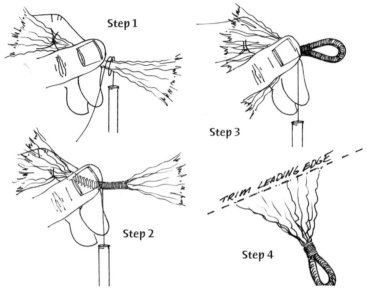

Step 1. Select a bundle of yarn half the diameter of the completed strike indicator. Pinch a little under half of the length of the bundle in your left hand. Trap the thread with your thumb and forefinger and begin wrapping.

Step 2. Once you have the thread started, grab both ends of the yarn and twirl the bobbin around the yarn like you would whip a loop on a fly line (see page 108). Wrap about ¾ of an inch—enough so that you can double it over to form a loop.

Step 3. Double over the material to form a loop and wrap over both ends with your thread. Secure the loop with a whip-finish.

Step 4. Trim the indicator and fluff with a brush. Pretreat indicators with floatant and let them dry.

Au Naturale

On heavily pressured waters—particularly in slow, flat areas—large, brightly colored indicators alert fish, and you'll see trout move away from indicator as it drifts toward them. In these areas, use small yarn indicators that land more softly than bobber types, and use off-white, dull-olive, or brown yarn to simulate natural debris floating on the water's surface.

Recycle Fly Line

Slide short lengths (¼ inch) of old fly line over a knot on your leader. These inexpensive indicators are especially good for small dry flies and midges, and you can reel them up through your guides. They sink if you use them with weighted flies, but if you use a brightly colored line, you can see them twitch when a fish strikes. Preparing your fly line is like stripping copper wire.

Step 1. Cut the line's coating (not the core) with a razor blade into 1-inch sections (you can always cut shorter after you strip them). It's easier to make them in batches.

Step 2. Soak the end of the line for up to 15 seconds in a container of nail-polish remover.

Step 3. Strip the vinyl coating from the core with your fingernails.

Step 4. Slide over a knot on your leader.

Step 1

Step 2

Step 3

Step 4

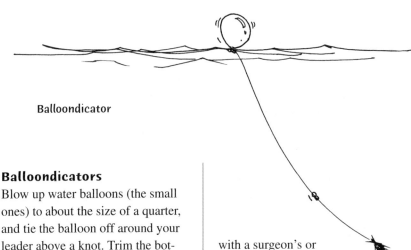

Balloondicator

Balloondicators

Blow up water balloons (the small ones) to about the size of a quarter, and tie the balloon off around your leader above a knot. Trim the bottom of the balloon. You can also trim the bottom of the balloon after you tie a knot in it, and then connect it to your leader with a slip knot. These are great for suspending heavy nymphs in fast currents and are very sensitive to strikes.

SPLIT SHOT

Wrap the tippet around the shot twice before crimping it shut to keep it from sliding down the leader and butting up against your fly.

Crimp it above a knot, if your shot still slides. If you don't have a knot at the right location, cut the tippet where you want the shot and retie it with a surgeon's or blood knot.

Never close or open shot with your teeth. Use forceps. Older split shot is made from lead, and you shouldn't put that in your mouth. Newer shot, though nontoxic, can still ruin your teeth.

Do not dispose of shot in the stream, especially lead shot. Instead, carry an empty film canister for waste such as shot and tippet.

For an instant jig, place a split-shot 1 to 3 inches up the tippet from a streamer such as a Woolly Bugger. The distance you place the shot from your nymph or streamer determines its action.

Shot

Putty and shot

Mold weighted putty around micro shot (or a knot in your leader) to help keep it in place. The warmer the putty, the easier it is to mold.

Add a few drops of vinegar and water to the bag and oxidation takes the sheen off shot in a few days. Some pressured fish spook at the glint of metallic shot.

DOUBLE-DUTY FORCEPS

Buy forceps with built-in scissors. You'll use the scissors for everything from trimming hackle—to change a bushy dry to a flush-floating one—trimming Glo Bug yarn on egg patterns, and making and trimming your own strike indicators.

THE APOTHECARY ANGLER

On your next trip to the drugstore, stock up on these essential items.

Alcohol wipes. Many drug stores and department stores sell inexpensive lint-free lens wipes treated with alcohol for cleaning sunglasses. Keep these on hand—in your glove box, fanny pack, vest, shirt pocket—for cleaning your sunglasses. One wipe cleans several pairs, so when you are cleaning yours, offer to clean your partners'.

Nail clippers. They often come with bead chain that you can use to fasten them to a zipper on your vest or fanny pack and work as well or better than any nipper you buy in a fly shop.

Diamond-dust nail files. Great for honing trout hooks.

Sally Hansen's Hard-As-Nails. Good fly-tying cement and for coating the thread wraps on your whipped loops.

Rubber gloves. For getting a grip on stuck rod pieces (see "Freeing Stuck Ferrules," page 120).

Rubbing alcohol and spray bottle. For finding leaks in waders (see "Pin-Hole Leaks," page 132).

Medical tape. To put on your stripping fingers to prevent blisters and cuts from a day of intense fishing.

Fishing first-aid kit. Keep lists and stock up on the items that you might need. Keep several kits around—a lightweight one for backpacking, one for the car, and one for the boat. Make sure to include Liquid Bandage—works great for cuts.

Krazy Glue. Keep in your first-aid kit for cuts or replacing a tip-top guide on your rod.

Dental-floss threader. Great for threading your fly-tying bobbins or using for a whip-finish on a whipped loop.

Orthodontic rubber bands. For Dick Galland's puffball nymphing rig (see page 135).

Assorted sewing needles. For Whitlock's Zap-A-Gap splice or tying needle knots on your leader.

Reading glasses. Inexpensive drug store reading glasses provide that extra bit of magnification you need for threading tippet at dusk.

BRAIDING WIRE

As an alternative to flexible wire leader material for bluefish, pike, and other toothy critters, buy braided wire in spools at your local craft store for much less.

MAKE YOUR OWN STRIPPING BASKET

Stripping baskets aren't just for the salt. They come in handy when you are moving from pool to pool on your favorite river and help keep your line away from tangles on brushy streams. Many tackle manufacturers sell stripping baskets, but you can make a few of them for under $10.

Materials

old wading belt, nylon strap with buckles, or bungee cord
dishpan or white bucket (Sterilite makes a good one)
cable ties (6-inch)
drill

Drill holes in the side of the dish pan to accommodate the hooks on your bungee cord. If you want to get fancy, cut slits in the plastic with a hot knife and insert a belt. Drill closely spaced holes in the bottom of the basket for the cable ties. Insert cable ties through adjacent holes and tighten. Depending on the basket depth, you may have to trim the cable ties, but don't trim them too much. Drill additional holes for drainage if you desire.

STRIPPING BASKET TIPS

Distribute the line evenly in the bottom of the basket.

A little water in the bottom of the basket helps reduce tangles.

Place the first few coils of line flat in the bottom of the basket. Don't just drop the line into the basket, make sure your hands touch the bottom of the basket or fingers. Loops that stick up often tangle.

If it's really windy, a deep basket often works better than a shallow one. Make a few different baskets for different conditions.

In a wind, move your basket downwind of your body, generally to one side or the other.

If you use a stripping basket in the surf, make sure there are enough large holes in the bottom for it to drain. You can modify plastic baskets (even store-bought ones) with a drill to make sure that the holes are big enough.

Homemade stripping basket

Watch Your Feet

When walking with a stripping basket, or not using it, put it behind you so that you can see your feet.

Retrofit your basket. The sky is the limit with retrofitting your basket. Some anglers use cable ties to secure bright foam (small-size pool noodle toys) around the lid to make it easier on the hands, help the basket float if it becomes separated from you, and make you more visible if it does not—the underside of the foam also makes a decent fly patch. If you don't like the belt that came with yours, swap it with another one.

Make a custom VLMD (vertical line management device) that collapses for storage from a lawn and leaf bag or a collapsible laundry hamper. George Anderson cuts the top off a collapsible leaf bucket (available in department stores) and puts a piece of plywood cut to shape in the bottom to keep it upright in a wind. He recommends trimming off any handles and other external items that could catch your line. The Rubbermaid version has Velcro straps to keep it flat while the boat is moving or while flying. A Ziploc bag with sand or rocks is weight enough and, unlike plywood, is disposable.

POLARIZED GLASSES

Good polarized glasses are an overlooked piece of fishing equipment, especially for intermediate to advanced fly fishers, who have learned to hunt fish rather than chuck flies and chance it. Buy quality glasses, and take care of them like you care for your rod and reel. Always wear a lanyard so you don't drop your investment in the drink. When matched to the correct lighting conditions, they can be a big help in spotting fish, plus sunglasses worn throughout the day reduce eye strain and fatigue that can give you headaches. Lens color and the amount of light that lens lets in should be determined by the type of fishing that you are going to be doing.

Choose the Right Lens

Darker tints are for bright conditions, lighter tints for variable or dark conditions, as a general rule.

Gray: Bright, sunny days and open-water fishing. Good glass for the salt.

Copper or brown: All-around lenses for trout fishing with good color contrast.

Amber/yellow: First and last light; heavily shaded streams; driving lenses to reduce glare from headlights at night on long road trips.

Get Side Shields

Most stylish glasses don't have them, but they help you see better and reduce eye strain.

Rain-X

Pretreat your sunglasses with Rain-X (simply wipe on clean, dry lenses, follow manufacturer's suggestions) if you spend a lot of time in a boat around open water. Many fishing lenses now come pretreated with a similar coating.

STAYING DRY

Purchase a light, packable raincoat for day trips. You are more likely to bring something that folds up in the back pocket of your vest or pack than a cumbersome jacket designed for extreme foul weather.

Pack dry bags when you take a trip on boats. You can't count on the boat having completely dry storage.

Wear wicking layers under your waders—even in the summer—to move perspiration quickly off of your body so you feel dry and comfortable. Sock liners, even in summer, keep your feet from feeling clammy.

Ziploc Bags

Carry a gallon-size Ziploc freezer bag for cameras, wallet, cell phone, and other items that can't get wet in your vest or pack—you never know when you might need temporary weatherproofing.

Waterproof is different than water-resistant. When you buy a heavy-duty raincoat, get one that is waterproof.

Treat your outerwear with Revivex or similar water repellant whenever water ceases to bead on it.

PART 3

Hatches
and Seasons

10

Hatches

COLOR CODE

In general, flies that hatch in the spring and fall have dark-colored backs, and flies that hatch in the summer, beginning with PMDs in the West and Sulphurs in the East, are light colored.

WHAT THE TROUT SEE

When matching an insect, consider the belly color rather than the back color—the belly is what trout see (at least on the floating adults). Most insects are either a shade of olivish brown or light cream/yellow

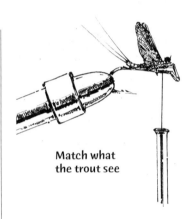

Match what
the trout see

on their undersides, and if you carry imitations in these two major colors, in the right size and profile, you can match most mayflies.

BACKLIGHTING

To detect spinners and other airborne bugs, look toward the sun. Insects are much easier to see when they are backlit.

USDA HARDINESS ZONE MAPS

Hardiness zone maps used for planting give you an idea of similar microhabitats. Catch a hatch later on streams in colder zones; earlier on streams in warmer zones. They are available for download from USDA (the National Arboretum) for state and country at http://www.usna .usda.gov/Hardzone/ushzmap.html. This one for the United States is from arborday.org/.

Look for Clues

S tonefly shucks on rocks indicate emerging stoneflies, swallows or other birds stitching the air may mean a hatch, inspect cobwebs for remnants of last night's hatch. Gasstation lights attract all sorts of bugs that hatch on rivers nearby.

2006 arborday.org Hardiness Zones Map

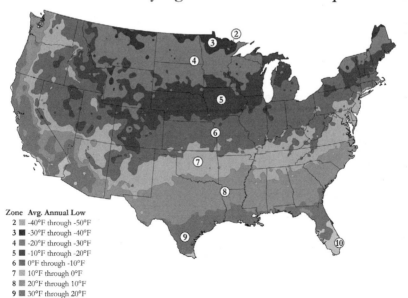

Zone	Avg. Annual Low
2	-40°F through -50°F
3	-30°F through -40°F
4	-20°F through -30°F
5	-10°F through -20°F
6	0°F through -10°F
7	10°F through 0°F
8	20°F through 10°F
9	30°F through 20°F
10	40°F through 30°F

Mastering the Hatches

Charles Meck

The recipe for catching trout during a hatch is one part timing, one part preparation, and a healthy dose of luck.

Carry several sizes of the same pattern. Always carry the size that most appropriately matches the hatch, but also carry smaller patterns.

Carry several patterns that match the same hatch. For the most common hatches, I carry Catskill-style, parachute, and Compara-dun style versions of the same fly.

Sink the pattern, if changing size or pattern doesn't work.

Move during the hatch if you don't see risers. Don't be afraid to drive or walk up or downstream. Sometimes fish tend to pod up; other times, water or hatch conditions vary in a stream from one area to the next.

Clockwise from left: Catskill-style, parachute, and Compara-dun

Arrive at the right time. Know when the bugs hatch and be there. In the spring, fall, and winter this is often midday; in the summer, plan to be on the water late.

Fish on lousy days. Aquatic insects that hatch on overcast days tend to remain on the surface longer than when they hatch on bright sunny days. Trout are also less wary and feed more readily on cloudy, overcast days.

Fish tandem flies. Cover multiple bases with multiple flies. Fish both the adult and emerger, or emerger and nymph, or another combination. (For more on fishing two-fly rigs, read *Fishing Tandem Flies* [Headwater Books, 2007].)

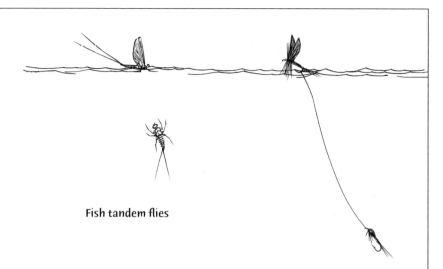

Fish tandem flies

Travel. Extend your fishing time for the super hatches—Green Drakes, for instance—by traveling from stream to stream, generally from south to north or from low to high elevation to follow the hatches at their peaks.

Location is everything. Sulphurs and drakes emerge in totally different areas of stream in different habitats. Drakes prefer silty bottoms; Sulphurs (and many other mayflies) prefer riffles. Learn and seek out the habitats different insects prefer.

Take time out to identify what is hatching. You don't need to know Latin, but sometimes a bug looks a different color or size up close than it does flying in the air. Take time to discern how fish are feeding on the insects: Are they boiling just under the surface or leaping out of the water? (See "Reading the Rise," page 154.)

Stonefly

Trico Time

John Barr

Tricorythodes *mayflies, Tricos for short, are one of the most widespread and predictable mayfly hatches in the country, occurring on many flowing waters from coast to coast. They can start hatching in late June and continue through October on a daily basis. Because they are so small and prolific, many fly fishers have trouble catching fish during a hatch.*

Trico duns usually hatch very early in the morning, sometimes in the dark. Unless you have some light on the water, the very small—generally size 20 and smaller—dun patterns can be difficult to see. Spinners are the most important stage to anglers because the spinner fall occurs later in the morning when the visibility is better, and trout love the easy meal of a dead spinner.

If trout are rising sporadically, they are probably feeding on the duns or some other insect. After the spinners hit the water's surface, the pace of the rising increases to a frenzied, rapid cadence. This is your tip that the trout are feeding on Trico spinners. Trout can get picky when feeding on Trico spinners, so you must have a good spinner pattern in the correct size.

The male Trico spinner is all black, and the female has a black thorax and pale-olive abdomen. I have heard of places where trout key on the two-toned females, but all-black patterns have always worked fine for me.

When the Tricos start hatching early in the season, they can be as large as a size 18. As the months progress, they get smaller and can be a size 26 or smaller in October. The density of the hatch and spinner fall also decreases as the months progress. Carry a good selection of sizes in your Trico box.

A dead drift is essential to success. Trico spinners are dead and motionless, and trout will not take a waking spinner. For years I fished a single floating spinner pattern. The small, flush-floating fly was difficult to see, and it was hard to tell if I was getting a drag-free drift.

Fish a Trico spinner fall with a floating, black-bodied Trico Vis-A-Dun, with a sunken spinner tied off the bend on 6 inches of 6X tippet. The Vis-A-Dun lets me know I am getting a drag-free drift, and with the grizzly hackle clipped on the bottom, it is regularly taken as a spinner. If a trout takes the drowned spinner, the Vis-A-Dun acts as a strike indicator.

Natural spinners may cover the surface and compete with a floating pattern. A drowned spinner stands out better.

When trout quit feeding on surface spinners, they often move to the heads of runs and feed on drowned spinners. In this situation, I fish a size 10 hopper, a size 18 black Copper John, and a drowned spinner combination and can usually count on an hour or two of good fishing.

I use 6X premium-grade fluorocarbon tippet when fishing spinners.

Trico clouds

BEAT THE BRUSH

To match the hatch, get a sample. Many types of hatching insects fly and rest in streamside vegetation. It's easier to ambush them there than capture them on the wing.

WATCH THE BIRDS

Birds such as waxwings and swallows (and a host of others) get active when bugs hatch. Even when you can't see them, bugs may be present if you see the birds dipping and darting in the air.

PRESENTATION IS KEY

Most of the time, on most of the streams throughout the United States, nothing is hatching. Trout have to be opportunistic feeders, and if your presentation is good and pattern imitates something a trout eats, you are ahead of the game.

READING THE RISE

Trout behave differently on different rivers, and though anglers over the years have tried to describe the nature of riseforms, we can do so only generally. Here are tips to help you figure out what the fish are feeding on. Use these clues along with other indicators, such as time of year, time of day, and visible insects.

Use a pair of binoculars to determine riseforms from afar.

   When trout are feeding on small flies, their riseforms are usually small with few splashes.

   Splashier rises tend to come from immature trout or fish chasing

Beat the brush

caddis or other fast-moving insects like damselflies and stoneflies.

Bulges or boils below the surface mean fish are feeding on emergers and indicate that an emerger, soft-hackle, or other wet is the best choice. Pay careful attention to rises to determine whether the riseform is from a fish feeding on or slightly below the surface.

Porpoising trout often show head, back, fins, and tail and tend to feed on emerging mayflies or midge pupae, and sometimes surface insects (look for bubbles). Sometimes you just see the back and not the head.

Sipping trout are feeding on small flies—mayfly emergers, spinners, small terrestrials such as bee-

Bulging rise

Porpoising trout

Porpoising trout (headless)

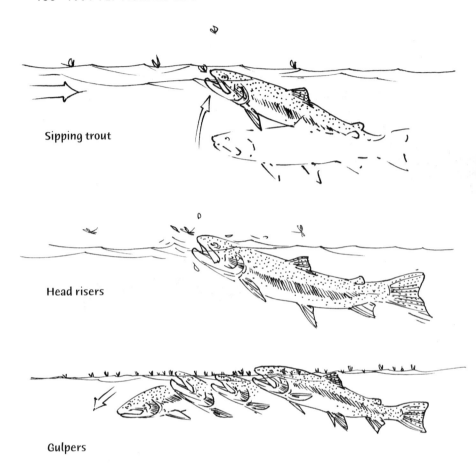

Sipping trout

Head risers

Gulpers

tles and ants—in the surface film or on the surface. These riseforms may also indicate fish are taking spinners in the surface film. On smooth water, the trout may leave a few small bubbles, but these rises are hard to detect in broken currents.

Head risers are feeding on insects at the surface and their heads come entirely out of the water. Unlike sipping risers, you can usually determine the size of a head riser by the size of the head and their wake. They leave behind telltale bubbles when returning to the water.

Gulpers are a breed of head risers, working on a faster rhythm, usually feeding on profuse hatches

Flying trout

Tailing trout

of insects on flat water, such as Trico spinner falls or *Callibaetis*. In slow-moving or still water, mark the direction gulpers are moving and place your fly in their path. Don't cast where they last rose.

Fish leaping out of the water are what Montana guide E. Neale Streeks calls "flying trout." Depend-

ing on time of year and time of day, this usually signifies fish taking caddis emergers or damselflies or dragonflies (midday in the summer).

Tailing trout. When trout root headfirst for cressbugs or scuds in bottom vegetation they often wave their tails in or slightly above the water like redfish.

Fishing Pods

George Anderson

Pods, large groups of feeding fish, provide exciting and demanding fishing.

Approach from below the pod. Accuracy is key, so get as close as you can. I often get within 15 to 20 feet of my target—close enough to observe the individual rises and feeding patterns of the fish.

Have a plan. If you cast into the pod, all the fish will spook and scatter. Strategize about how to catch as many fish as possible. That may mean picking off fish at the tail of the pod or fish feeding off to the side. If you are not after numbers, stalk the largest trout.

Pick steady risers. Don't waste your time on sporadic risers, unless they are large.

Many trout rise at regular intervals. Predict when the trout will rise and time your casts accordingly.

Focus on individuals. Don't cast into the group and hope that one eats your fly.

Don't waste too much time on one fish. If I can't get a trout to take after a half-dozen good casts, I pick another target.

If you have tricky surface currents, change your casting position slightly or put more slack in the leader and tippet by mending or using a slack-line, pile, or curve cast.

For utmost accuracy, I drive the line directly over the rod tip on the forward cast so that the leader and tippet lay out straight toward the fish, rather than hooking or slicing in at an odd angle.

Most anglers cast too far upstream of the fish. The fly should land between 8 and 15 inches ahead of the fish and on a path that will take it directly over its nose.

Seeing small flies can be difficult, but if you cast a straight line, you should know approximately where your fly is on the surface. If you see a fish rise within a foot or two of that spot, set the hook.

Sometimes I fire the fly at the surface a little harder than normal to make it easier for me to see where the fly hits the water. Slamming down a spinner can make it sink a little, and submerged spinners are very effective.

When you hook a fish, the best scenario is that it peels away from the pod. If it runs into the pod, I immediately slack off pressure to calm it and prevent it from cartwheeling through the pool. When the fish heads back downstream, I apply the heat and move it away from the pod.

Sometimes you can't help but put down the pod after hooking a fish. Be patient. After 10 minutes or so, the pod usually starts feeding again.

A pecking order in most pods puts the largest fish up front. Going for Mr. Big by casting over his buddies won't work. Get above the pod and drift your fly downstream with a combination of a reach cast and mending. Your first casts are critical.

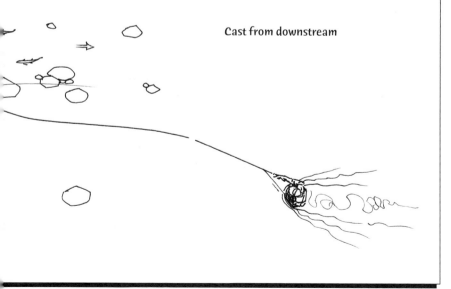

Cast from downstream

Tips for Catching Selective, Rising Trout

Mike Lawson

Many consider casting to selective trout rising to hatching insects the essence of fly fishing, but it can be frustratingly difficult.

Time spent studying a trout's feeding rhythm is often more productive than repeatedly casting over the same trout. Your best chance is your first cast.

If you don't know what fly to use, study the water with binoculars or use a small insect net to seine the water close by. Select a fly that is the approximate size and color of the natural.

Get Close

Getting close reduces the need to false-cast, and the closer you are, the more accurate your casts.

Although you may know what insect a trout is eating, you must determine whether it is feeding on, in, or just under the surface film. You can determine if the fish is feeding on or in the surface by watching individual insects with binoculars as they drift over the feeding fish.

When you approach a rising trout, wade as quietly and carefully as possible so you don't make too much disturbance in the water and to minimize the sound of your wading boots grinding against the bottom. **After you get** into position, wait for the trout to rise a couple of times before you make your first cast.

If you put a trout down and it stops feeding, stay in position and wait 5 minutes or so. It will often start feeding again. Don't forget to look around. Sometimes a spooked fish will change locations and start rising again.

Draw the trout's attention to your fly—if the surface is covered with aquatic insects—by giving it a subtle twitch just as it starts to enter the trout's window of vision.

When you need to use a small fly or emerger to match the hatch, you can attach the small hatch-matching pattern as a dropper 8 to 12 inches from a larger fly.

Unmatch the Hatch

If the surface is covered with aquatic insects, sometimes you need to use something different like a Royal Wulff, Parachute Adams, or beetle to draw the trout's attention. It should be about the same size as the naturals.

11

Seasons

SPRING
The Phenological Fly
Mayfly hatches coincide with bloom periods of common trees and flowers. Learn to recognize these patterns and record them in a journal.

Hatch-matcher Charles Meck first planted the seed of this idea in *Great Rivers, Great Hatches.* Canadian Bob Scammell contributed to the body of knowledge of Western hatches with *The Phenological Fly.*

For example, in Pennsylvania, blooming forsythia or wild ginger indicate that anglers should be on the lookout for Hendricksons, blooming mountain laurel signifies Slate Drake time, and wild rhododendron, Tricos. According to Scammell, sighting brown-eyed Susans mean *Hexagenia* are emerging, and at the first signs of clematis blooms, he starts looking for Western March Brown in his neck of the woods, Alberta.

When watching plants and flowers, wild specimens are best because microhabitats near houses and in suburban gardens can expedite bloom times.

Hunter-Gatherer

Even catch-and-release anglers can show their spouses that time spent wandering in the woods is not in vain. In the spring, hunt for morels and gather fiddleheads, which are delicacies at the table.

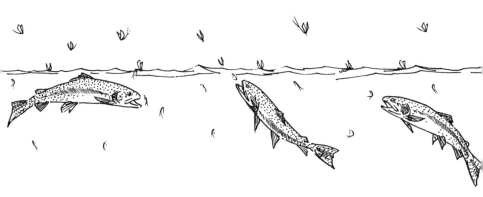

Splat Tactics

When casting inchworms, beetles, hoppers, and other terrestrials, don't be bashful about splatting the fly on the surface of the water. The naturals often fall into the water less than gracefully, and the disturbance attracts fish.

Runoff

Spring means runoff, but different streams will be in different stages. Learn what streams drop and clear quicker than others to maximize your fishing time. These streams may also clear faster after a summer rainstorm.

Fish When It's Warmest

In the spring, most mayflies hatch in the midafternoon into evening.

Go Deep in Colder Water

In general, higher, colder water means less surface activity. Fish streamers and nymphs more frequently in the spring or hang a nymph dropper off of your dry fly.

Fish Eggs

Suckers and rainbow trout spawn in the spring, so egg patterns can be effective.

Henry's
Fork Hopper

SUMMER
Trico Time
Summer's main game is Tricos in the morning, but you can fish terrestrials midday and find rising fish near dark. For the brave of heart, night fishing (see page 47) offers shots at big browns.

Terrestrial Tactics
Size down your hoppers.
Fly shops sell a lot of large hopper patterns, but naturals come in all sizes and smaller patterns may surprise fish.

On many streams, crickets are a wise alternative to hoppers. Anglers don't fish cricket patterns as much as hoppers, yet they are as abundant, even more so in wooded areas.

Cricket

Sink any terrestrial with split shot or tie some weighted ones ahead of time. Trout are suckers for sunken hoppers, inchworms, and ants.

Stealth Flies
Low water makes it easier to find fish and to wade about, but also makes fish warier. Trade heavy-hackled spring patterns for flush-floating ones.

Anticipate Ants
Flying ants migrate in late summer and fall, and often fall into the water, causing periods of feeding frenzy. These migrations are often predictable, so ask around. Carry simple Antron- or CDC-winged patterns in your box.

Fish Faster Water
Look for fish in faster, more oxygenated water. Wet wade to find the spring holes where fish congregate in warmer water temperatures. Note these spots for your winter fishing as well.

Seek the Shade
Seek out and fish in the shade—whether entire pools, or shaded spots in a particular pool. Don't spend too much time on water baking in the sun. Bridges are always a good bet.

Sun and Mosquitoes

Baseball caps are popular fly-fishing headgear, but they do a poor job of protecting your head and neck from the sun. Carry a bandana and tuck it under the back of your cap if you are out in the sun; wet it for cool relief on a hot day.

Long-sleeve shirts are warmer than short-sleeve shirts, but they protect your arms from sun and bugs a lot better.

Wear lightweight Capilene or polypro long underwear under your breathable waders in the summer to help transfer sweat and keep you from feeling clammy. Plus, they add a layer of warmth if you are wading in colder tailwaters. Air temps may be hot, but the water may not.

Apply sunscreen before you go fishing, and wash your hands. When you reapply it regularly through the day, apply it with the back of your hand so that you don't get it on your fly line. Put on your bug dope before fishing as well—after you apply the sunscreen. Most experts agree that you should buy individual and not combination products.

Carry lip balm with you and use it regularly to protect your lips from burning.

Drink lots of water through the day—at least two quarts. If you're taking a long trip but can't carry a lot of water, drink lots on the car ride to your fishing spot.

Do not put sunblock on your forehead—it can drip into your eyes (wear a hat to protect that part of your face). Even if the bottle says its tearproof, sweatproof, waterproof, it probably is not. Baby sunblocks are most likely to be tear-free. Use SPF 30 or higher.

Many saltwater flats guides wear thin balaclavas over their faces and gloves on their hands, trading the mild discomfort of additional clothing for the enhanced protection against the sun.

Don't get DEET on your fly line

Lightning Tips

According to the National Oceanic and Atmospheric Administration (NOAA) National Weather Service, approximately 1,800 thunderstorms are occurring at any given time, about 16 million thunderstorms each year. Most thunderstorms last about 30 minutes and are typically about 15 miles (24 km) in diameter.

Count the seconds (one thousand one, one thousand two) between seeing the lightning and hearing the first sound of thunder and divide by 5 to get the approximate distance of the storm in miles. Sound in the atmosphere travels just under a mile in 5 seconds.

Sharply defined streaks of lightning are probably close. If you see a flash but not bolts, the storm is likely farther away. Sharp, abrupt thunderclaps are very close; rumbles farther away.

To determine storm size, follow the steps for determining the distance, but continue counting as long as you can hear the faint rumblings of thunder. Subtract this number from the number you got when calculating the distance of the storm based on the first sound of thunder for the storm's approximate size.

Avoid water, high ground, open spaces, all metal objects including fences, machinery, motors, and large natural objects such as trees and boulders that can attract lightning.

Seek safety in a large building (preferably one with steel girders) or a car (with windows completely shut). The metal frame conducts electrical charge and passes it along to the ground. If lightning strikes a tree, the charge can transmit through the ground through the roots, so don't seek safety under a tree. Some experts say that if the tree is your only option, then pick one with a deep root system, such as an oak tree.

If lightning strikes nearby when you are outside, crouch down, place your hands over your ears to minimize hearing damage from thunder, and stay at least 15 feet away from other people.

If out in a boat, stay in the center of the cabin if you can. If there is no cabin, stay low in the boat. Keep arms and legs in the boat and out of the water. Stop fishing and put down your rods and anything else you might have in your hands. Do not talk on your cell phone. Disconnect electronic equipment and lower antennae.

FALL

Water in the fall is typically low and clear, and fish have had a season's education about the latest fly patterns. You must have excellent presentations and approach.

Most fish species feed heavily to prepare for winter and streams are less crowded, making fall an ideal time to be on the water.

Brown and brook trout spawn in the fall, so you may catch aggressive and territorial males if you fish streamers.

Steelhead ascend rivers with fall rains

Stand Out

Wear at least one article of fluorescent-orange clothing when fishing during hunting season. Fall is not the time to blend in with your environment.

Bring a fleece jacket or a parka even if the weather forecast is nice. Fall weather can change quickly.

Fish feed earlier in the day, like in spring.

Flies are dark in the fall and dry fly selections relatively simple: out West, *Baetis,* October Caddis, and Tricos can be important; in the East, *Baetis,* Tricos, and *Isonychia* are important.

Sculpin

WINTER
Flat-Water Risers
If you are looking for risers on a nice winter day, concentrate on flat water in pools as well as shallow water that warms quickly.

Small Flies
Cold-weather bugs are almost always small and mostly midges. In late winter and early spring, *Baetis* and black stoneflies can hatch, but they are also small. Fill your winter box with mostly small subsurface patterns, a few dry flies for those opportunities when they arise, and a few meat-and-potatoes flies such as stonefly nymphs and streamers. Egg patterns are also excellent choices.

Slow and Low
The colder the water, the deeper and slower you should fish your fly. Fish won't move far to take streamers, so try dead-drifting them under an indicator. Break the water into rows and methodically fish each one.

Spring Creeks and Tailwaters
Focus on springs creeks and tailwaters, which don't freeze in the winter and have more stable water temperatures.

Don't Leave Fish to Find Fish
Winter fish tend to pod up, so if you catch one, don't move to a better spot. You're probably in it.

Ice-Free Guides
Chapstick, Vaseline, or cooking spray on your guides reduces the amount of ice build-up.

Fish Smarter
Once the guides ice up, use roll and Spey casts to fish as much as possible without stripping in line. With these casts, you can also keep your hands toasty in mittens.

Think Spring
Springs entering a river keep water cool in the summer and ice free in the winter.

Staying Warm

The key to staying safe in the winter (and enjoying yourself).

Don't go into the water if you don't have to.

Bring a spare set of clothes and keep them in your vehicle for emergencies. Carry a waterproof case of strike-anywhere matches in case you need to build a fire.

Boot-foot waders are warmer than stocking foots because they are generally less constricting and allow more circulation. Regardless of boot type, make sure there's room in your boots and your feet aren't constricted. Wool and most other materials provide insulation by trapping warm air in the spaces and in the fibers. If your wading boots are too tight, even good socks can't perform their function.

Breathable waders are fine in winter—if you layer properly. Start with a thin, tight base layer that wicks moisture and keeps your skin dry and then add one or two layers of fleece pants—depending on the air and water temperature. Your waders should keep your lower body warm under all but the most severe conditions. Wear thin sock liners and good socks.

A warm fleece or wool hat under the hood of your wading jacket can keep you warm on cold days. An exposed head loses body heat quickly. If you get warm in the afternoon, your hat may be the only layer you need to remove.

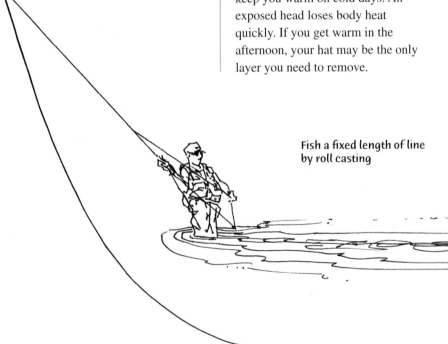

Fish a fixed length of line by roll casting

Warm packs designed for boots and gloves provide a quick source of heat (Grabber Mycoal is one popular brand).

Bring two or three pairs of wool, fleece, or neoprene fingerless gloves on cold winter days. Leave an extra pair of mittens in the car just in case. An extra pair of dry gloves in your vest can keep you fishing after everyone else goes home. Stuff some inexpensive liner gloves into your vest or pack. They don't take up space, but you'll appreciate the spare set if you get your main gloves wet or leave them at home.

Bloodflow to your feet and hands decreases when your core body temperature decreases. Keep your extremities warm by properly layering your torso and legs to keep your core body temperature warm.

Sole Savvy

Felt soles collect snow and become cumbersome and dangerous. Sticky rubber soles— such as the Aquastealth brand— with studs are best.

Eat lots of protein, carbohydrates, and fats. You need to keep the fires stoked to stay warm. Bring along a thermos of your favorite hot beverage. Prime it by pouring boiling water into it and letting that sit for 10 minutes or so before dumping it out and putting in your drink.

Save the alcohol until you're inside. We feel cold when blood flows from our skin into the organs to keep our core temperature warm. After drinking alcohol, blood flows to the skin (making us feel warm and our faces flush), which makes our core body temperature decrease rapidly.

Frosty Freestoners

Joe Cambridge

Anglers usually head for spring creeks or tailwaters in the winter, if they head out at all. But freestone streams can also provide some good winter fishing.

Mid morning to early afternoon is the magic window—when it's the warmest—so sleep late and be off the water long before supper.

Carry a variety of nymphs and midge pupa imitations—most of the action will be subsurface.

Ruffed grouse can sometimes provide clues to the whereabouts of winter trout. Seeking protection from the elements, the birds often pick spots where heavy pine cover reduces wind chill and spring water seeps from the ground. Note the places where you flush grouse regularly, and carefully work any holes or holding areas just downstream of these areas.

Walk or cross-country ski on days when fishing is impossible to note any open water, which are likely locations of springs. Binoculars help you search terrain without trudging through snow.

Find the Fish

Look for spots where water temperatures are highest and current speeds are more suited to a trout's slow metabolism at this time of year. Bridge holes where steady sun warms the concrete and nearby water are good bets.

Don't fish your favorite bamboo or most expensive graphite stick. Use a rod you won't miss if the worst happens. Falls are not uncommon in snow and ice. Should you slip, you're likely to go to your strong hand to catch yourself, so learn to carry your rod in the weak hand and keep the tip pointed behind you.

Avoid standing in one place for too long in cold water. When you decide to move, your legs won't work well, and next comes the unpleasant, dangerous bath. Force yourself to get out and move around once in a while to keep the circulation going.

Avoid crunching or collapsing the thin layer of ice lining the shore on your approach. Such noise carries a long way and alerts trout to your presence.

Timing Is Everything

Fish during the warmest part of the day; fish in the warmest water.

If the sun is out, stay back from the bank, especially if you're seeing "soot flies," the little stoneflies that look like wood ashes come alive. Even a pale-winter sun can get them hatching. Never splash through the shallows of a deep hole. Large trout sometimes hold in the sun-warmed shallows in water barely deep enough to cover their dorsals. They're not just there to keep warm; they are hunting the small, dark stoneflies scuttling out of the creek.

Carry binoculars so you can look for feeding trout without having to trudge through the snow. Even better, you may be able to scan the water from the comfort of your vehicle.

PART 4

Travel, Destinations, and Species Other Than Trout

12

Travel, Destinations, and Species Other Than Trout

GENERAL TRAVEL TRIPS

Use a checklist. Print one out, or save different ones for each fishing trip, especially if boating or camping. Create your own list on a computer and revise as necessary. Depending on your needs, you might prepare one for overseas travel, boat trips, saltwater trips, and so on.

Even on short trips, always put a spare rod in the car in case you break your main one.

Hide your keys near the car rather than carrying them with you to the

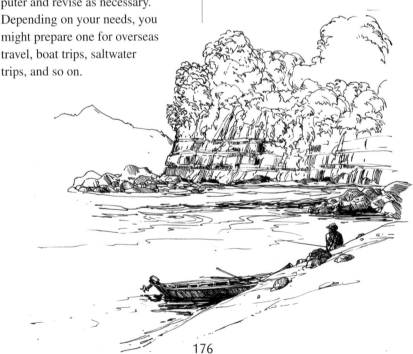

river. Tell your fishing buddy where they are in case of an emergency.

Don't plan on cell-phone coverage. Always tell someone where you are going or leave a note.

Purchase trip insurance that includes medical and medical evacuation insurance when traveling out of the country.

Rent a satellite phone for trips out of the country and hope you never have to use it. They are affordable insurance where cell phones don't work.

Buy licenses ahead of time online or over the phone through each state's fish and game department.

Keep your license in the same place, with equipment you always take fishing.

Tape inventory lists to your gear-storage boxes (Rubbermaid containers work well). That way you know what you have and what you need to replace in each box (this also works well for camping and cooking gear).

If possible, ship important gear to your destination ahead of time. That way, by the time you leave, you know your gear is waiting there for you, safe and sound.

DO YOUR HOMEWORK

Before you take a trip, whether it is to a new lodge 1,000 miles away or a closer jaunt, it pays to do a little research.

New School

Fly-fishing websites such as flyfisherman.com or danblanton.com have a treasure trove of information on them, so they are often a good place to begin searching for information. Before posting a question on the bulletin boards, remember to search through the archive of posts if the website has one. You don't want to ask a question that has already been answered, if you can help it.

Other recreational sites also provide information about fishing or water conditions. Many die-hard fly fishers monitor gear-fishing websites for fishing news. Surfing sites, for instance, provide information on

Online Mapping

Websites are great for trip planning. You can view satellite maps of a stream on many different websites such as Google Earth (earth.google.com) or terraserver.com.

ocean water conditions. Canoe or kayak websites often provide good information about boat launches or popular floats.

USGS streamflow data (water-data.usgs.gov/nwis) provides the best online resource for water conditions. Only familiarity with local water conditions will help you decipher the flow's impact on water clarity and other conditions, but in time and with practice, you'll be able to check streamflow to gauge the fishing conditions.

Bookmark your favorite weather website such as weather.com, and be sure to check it frequently before a trip. Compare past to predicted weather to identify trends that can affect fishing.

Old School

Purchase a *Delorme Atlas and Gazetter* for your state and other states that you fish frequently, and keep it in the car. Write notes on the map or on sticky notes.

Don't forget how helpful libraries can be. You can order magazine article reprints from Interlibrary Loan (if your library doesn't carry the magazine), which is often easier (and cheaper) than trying to find a back issue another way.

Being able to read a topographic map is an invaluable skill for fly fishers. With a basic understanding, you can look at a topo map of an area and reliably predict the character of the stream—as well as the nature of access. The narrower the lines, the steeper the ascent. Contour lines form V shapes in valleys or along stream beds. The point of the V points uphill.

Verify any information you glean from books, articles, fly-shop owners, and online bulletin boards with another source. Buy several guidebooks and compare them; call a fly shop after reading a report online. There is some flat-out bad information out there; but more often, people just have different experiences and opinions, so it helps to gather as much info as you can before embarking on your trip. Have realistic expectations. Some people really exaggerate fishing conditions and fish size.

Solicit local advice, but use your own common sense.

BEAR AWARE

Drowning presents a greater threat to fly fishers, but fishing several of the world's best fly-fishing destination involve sharing the water with bears. Here are some tips to prevent unpleasant encounters.

Carry bear spray in an accessible spot such as on your wading belt or pack shoulder strap, especially if you are fishing in grizzly country. Arrange to purchase it at your destination if you are flying because airlines don't allow it, even if it is packed in baggage.

Practice with the bear spray at least once by discharging some of it. This will give you some indication of how far and wide the spray travels. Follow manufacturer's instructions.

GUIDES

Even for experts, good guides are worth the expense because they can show you how to fish unfamiliar water, they often have a boat, they often have access to private water or know of less crowded areas, and they can arrange transportation and gear if you are traveling on business and want to get in a day of fishing. But you have a right to make sure you get what you pay for.

Unless you ask them to, good guides don't fish while they are working.

The best guides are good teachers. Tell them what you'd like to learn, and listen to what they have to tell you.

Be honest about your abilities right up front with the guide. They'll find out soon enough and honesty will save some embarrassing moments.

Have realistic expectations. Be fair to yourself and your guide. Your guide should work hard for you, but some days just weren't meant to be.

If you have special dietary requirements, tell the guide well in advance, not just before the drift-boat launches.

Before you book the trip, ask about tips, meals, transportation to and from the launch, how long you fish each day, who provides flies, etc.

Avoid surprising a bear. Make noise, especially where the sound of the flowing water can muffle your approach. Walk and camp in larger groups when in bear country. Wear a bear bell or sing while you walk, especially around blind corners.

When bears are also fishing nearby, such as on many Alaska streams, always give them plenty of room. If a bear approaches you, stop fishing and move away. Give a splashing fish slack, or cut the line, if the bear is interested in it.

Keep a clean camp. That means nothing but ashes in your fire pit, no food or water in your tent, hang a bear bag at least 50 yards from

Some guides provide lunch and drinks; others do not. In Florida, for instance, it is customary for you to provide your guide's drinks and lunch. **Don't let the number** of fish you catch solely determine the size of your tip. **On group trips** you may have to rotate guides. Some anglers like this and others do not. While it takes a while to learn how to communicate with your guide, some anglers don't want to get stuck with the same guide (especially one they don't mesh with) for the entire time. Understand how the guide/client rotation works *before* you go to a lodge or on a group trip. Also, keep an open mind: just because you don't have the lodge's best guide for the day doesn't mean you won't have good fishing and/or get along well with the guide that you do have.

The best guides are good teachers

your camp, don't clean fish near camp, stand upwind when cooking food to prevent your clothes from smelling like food, and other commonsense practices to avoid enticing trouble. Bears like food and are attracted by the smell, so don't encourage them.

Steer Clear Of

Bear cubs. Mothers may be nearby.

Dead animals such as elk, deer, cattle, etc. Grizzlies are protective of their food and may be nearby.

Feeding grounds such as berry fields (black and grizzly) or stands of whitebark pine trees (grizzly).

Backcountry Fishing

Ross Purnell

Put some distance between you and the crowds for the best fishing.

Preventing Dehydration

Drink at least 64 ounces of water per day when you are hiking or fishing. In hot weather or long hikes, you will use twice that much. Water is heavy, and filter systems are slow when you are thirsty. Use water-treatment drops (Aquamira or similar) to kill bacteria in water that is otherwise clear and drinkable. It's a tasteless treatment that saves weight and allows you to drink as much as you want. (Iodine tablets leave a bad taste in the water.)

Don't carry your multipiece rod in an aluminum tube. It adds weight, bulk, and makes it hard to attach to the outside of your pack. Carry your 3-, 4-, or 5-piece rod in the sock, strapped to the side of your pack. As long as the rod is secured properly, and the pack is longer than the unassembled rod pieces, the bulk of the pack will protect the rod.

Always hike with a buddy in the backcountry. Let someone know where you'll be hiking and fishing and when you are expected to return. Cell phones have limited coverage in remote areas so don't expect them to work.

Bring a hand-held GPS device along with your standard maps so you always know your position. You can determine the coordinates of your fishing destination beforehand using Google Earth, TravelByGPS.com, or a similar online application.

Leave the waders at home and plan on wet wading if you plan on hiking long distances in the warm summer months. Waders are too bulky and heavy to be worth the effort for a day trip, and are also impractical for overnight trips when you also must pack a tent, sleeping bag, and food.

Never wear cotton outdoors

Once it is wet, it stays wet— wet cotton is heavy and cold and a recipe for hypothermia. Avoid cotton (even cotton underwear) especially when wet wading, when hiking long distances to fish, or when you'll be camping in the backcountry. Your wet cotton clothing will not be dry in the morning.

Wear two pairs of socks for hiking and wet wading. Liner socks should be made from a thin, tight, synthetic material that wicks moisture out. This buffer layer protects your skin from blisters. Women's ankle-high pantyhose socks are a cheap alternative to brand-name liner socks.

Wear a thick, cushioning outer sock like heavyweight Capilene or SmartWool to help protect your feet at friction points including the back of your heel or the outside of your big toe. A two-sock system protects against blisters even when your shoes are soaked from wading.

Hiking in felt-soled wading boots is dangerous and will quickly wear out your soles. You'll be hiking more than wading, so wear lightweight hikers with stiff soles and aggressive treads.

continued on page 184

Backcountry Fishing continued

Layering is lightweight and more comfortable through a greater temperature range. Instead of a single heavy warm jacket, wear a tight synthetic base layer (cool when worn alone, dry and warm when layered). Bring a fleece and a water- and windproof jacket for an outer layer.

To ensure a warm sleep in a lightweight sleeping bag, use a closed-cell foam mattress or self-inflating mattress, and bring a lightweight polypropylene hat for sleeping. These two items are lighter and will keep you more comfortable than a bulky four-season sleeping bag.

Keep your fishing stuff—fly boxes, sunglasses, reel—in your pack's outside pockets. It's not uncommon to stop along the way on many hiking/fishing trips, and it can be frustrating if your fishing gear is at the bottom of your pack.

Simplify

Create a single fly box with flies suited for mountain streams and high lakes. Parachute Adams (#10–20), CDC & Elks (#14–16), foam beetles (#12–14), and foam ants (#16–20) are all you need in most alpine areas.

Aluminum-tipped trekking poles take some strain off your ankles and knees on rugged hikes and also make good wading staves.

Many national parks and other wilderness preserves do not allow fires. Stoves—along with the associated cookware—are cumbersome. On short one- or two-night trips, eat ready-to-eat, high-energy foods like beef jerky, energy bars, granola bars, and trail mix, nuts, and candy. This saves time so you can fish more, and saves space so you can pack extra fishing gear. Drink plenty of water with dehydrated foods like jerky and dried fruit.

Saltwater Travel Tips

Lefty Kreh

Many saltwater trips involve travel far afield and new tackle for lots of trout fishers.

Contact the locals. Before you make firm plans, call the guide, outfitter, or lodge you are fishing with and get updates on conditions.

Do your research. Ask guides and lodges for a list of references and call their references. Good guides should have a long list, not just a few names. Ask others who have fished the location who the best guides are, and try to get those guides. Request top guides in advance. Read as much as you can about your destination online, in magazines, or books.

Travel during the best times. Many fly-fishing destinations have peak periods of prime fishing. Plan to go at those times.

Know the tides. Tide has everything to do with the habits of fish. Research tides in advance, so you can plan for the best fishing.

When in a boat, always put on your raingear before motoring out. I prefer bib-type pants; regular rain pants can slip down when you sit, exposing your bottom and waist to rain and sea spray.

Copy your passport. Make several copies of the first page of your passport and store them separate from the original. If your passport is stolen or lost, you will have the information you need to get a replacement.

A waterproof bag for your valuables and items that can't get wet (cell phone, wallet, snack, digital camera) is invaluable if you will be spending any time in a boat, especially a moving boat when water splashes up and over the bow. Put the bag in a boat's dry storage for extra protection.

Consider other species. Be prepared to fish for species other than the ones you set out to catch because conditions are not always favorable. On a billfish trip I took, for example, the billfish were not around, so I fished a light, 8-weight fly rod and caught small tuna, rainbow runners, jacks, dolphin, and several other species. I had a ball.

Plan on Bad Weather

It is going to be hotter than they say, colder than they say, wetter than they say, and someone will forget the lunch. Bring the clothes you need to be comfortable in any weather.

Bring travel spin- or plug-casting gear. Some days will be so windy, you'll be better off sitting on the dock than trying to cast a fly line. I'd rather fish with spinning gear than sit around.

Use sun protection. Take an extra hat, spare polarized sunglasses, and plenty of strong sunscreen. Long-sleeved shirts designed for the tropics can reduce your exposure to the sun without making you feel uncomfortable. Consider wearing sungloves if you burn easily. Apply sunscreen several times daily. Keep sunscreen off your fingertips and palms of your hands because many sunscreen products can damage fly lines.

Pack wisely. Carry two bags and pack half of what you need in each bag. If one is lost or misdirected, the other will provide enough to fish with. Luggage tags tear off, so use duffel-type bags and label your name and address (not your phone number) on the side. Carry your reading materials, tickets, and other valuables in a backpack to keep your hands free.

Think comfort. Pack comfortable clothes for your trip, and also make sure that you have the medications and first-aid items that you need such as allergy pills, heartburn medicine, Imodium, aspirin, and lip balm. Pack things like tacky gauze tape, bandages, or a finger sock to protect the index finger of your rod hand when you are stripping line or fighting fish. Bring extra prescription glasses or contacts.

Flats Fishing

Lefty Kreh

Sight-fishing to flats species such as bonefish is exciting, but you need to be prepared for success.

Keep a clean line. Clean your line before you go out each day, and carry a line-cleaning kit with you in the boat for lines that have become sticky with salt. In a pinch you can use a cloth and fresh water to wipe the salt gum off a line.

Wear footwear that doesn't catch your fly line. I have often seen a cast fouled in midflight because the shooting line tangled in a shoe string. Many go barefoot, wear socks (to prevent burning), or wear slip-on shoes or sandals without laces.

Keep a clean boat. Whether you are with a guide or out on your own, keep the deck and general boat clean from anything that can catch your line or get in your way when you are fighting and landing a fish.

Clean Your Shoes

Wash your shoe soles in the water before entering the boat. Most guides hate it when anglers track dirt into their boats. Make sure your footwear has nonskid soles.

Stretch all coils from the line before making the first cast. Coils rob you of distance, are prone to tangling, and make it hard to efficiently set the hook.

Strip only the amount of line you need to cast to a fish. Too many anglers step up on the casting platform and then pull off 70 to 80 feet of line when they only need 50 to 60 feet. Any extra line on the deck is potential trouble. Master permit angler Del Brown figures 50 feet of line and a 10-foot leader is all he'll need for most situations. He makes a foot-long mark on the fly line at 50 feet. When he steps up to the casting platform, he strips off line until he reaches that mark.

Cast the line you have stripped from the reel and then retrieve it onto the boat deck. When you strip line from the reel, the forward end of the line falls to the bottom of the pile. Your last strip ends up on top of the pile. When you cast, the forward line comes from the bottom of the pile and tangles.

Keep line from underfoot. Casts are often ruined because you are stepping on your line. Stand a little back from the bow and drop the shooting in the well or on the main deck below the casting platform. You can also use a Line Tamer or a stripping basket, especially on windy days.

Don't stare at one spot when you search for fish. Constantly shift your eyes when you search the shallows. By staring at one place, you fail to see tiny wakes, moving fish, skipping minnows, and tailing fish. Use your peripheral vision.

Use your rod to locate the fish that the guide points out. When the guide says that the fish is at 10 o'clock (see "Telling Time," page 34) point the rod in that direction. The guide can tell you to move left or right. Before you head out to the flats, discuss with the guide how you will communicate—the clock system coupled with the rod-pointing system works well.

Don't cast until you see the fish. Unless the guide insists, never throw your fly where you think the fish is. This almost always results in a bad cast. Wait until you can spot your target.

Spare the guide. Know where the guide is when you are casting. If a fish is at 12 o'clock, don't cast until the guide has moved the rear of the boat to the side. If you cast straight ahead you will almost always hook the guide—not a good idea!

If the fish obviously doesn't see the fly, cast again. Most flats fish are sight-feeders; if you make a cast behind or too far to one side of the fish, don't continue to retrieve. Quietly pick up and cast again.

Strike by sweeping the rod sideways or with a strip-strike. Don't lift the rod tip when a fish grabs the fly. If the fish misses the fly, you've missed the strike and you may pull the fly out of the water. With a side or strip-strike, the fly remains in the water and you give the fish another chance to take it.

Beaches and Jetties

Bob Popovics

Simple strategies for the surf.

Keep it simple. The less you carry, the easier it is to walk from spot to spot, the easier it is to cast, and you are less tired at the end of the day. In New Jersey, where I fish most often, and throughout the East Coast, must-haves are a stripping basket, Korkers, bootfoot waders (stockingfoots don't keep sand out), good rain parka, polarized glasses (which also protect your eyes from stray flies), and your rod and reel. I like to store flies and other items in the large pockets on the outside of my jacket, rather than carry large bags and other things to hold tackle.

Good flies for bluefish are Bob's Bangers and chartreuse/white Surf Candies; for stripers, Bucktail Deceivers (black for night fishing, red/white during the day); and for albies, chartreuse/white Jiggies and Surf Candies.

Coil your shooting heads on wide-arbor tippet spools (such as Triple-fish Saltwater Leader) and then store the spools on your wader straps.

Ride the Wave

When you get the fish into the surf, use the water to help you land the fish quickly. Pull as the fish comes up the wave, keeping his head toward, not broadside, the beach.

Watch for people. If you are fishing on beaches or jetties, there will always be other people around. Conventional gear fishermen and other beachgoers are often not aware of how much room fly fishers need behind them. Always watch your backcast.

Ditch the rod and grab the line once you get the fish in close on a jetty. Too many anglers try to bring the fish to the rocks with their rod, which generally results in breaking the rod because of the poor angle. Put the rod down and control the fish with the line to prevent broken rods.

Take your stripping basket off or put it behind you when walking on the jetty so that you can see the gaps in between the rocks and other hazards.

Use different baskets for different conditions. No one stripping basket can do it all. For fishing in the surf or from a jetty, I like deep stripping baskets with large, quarter-size holes in the bottom to drain water quickly. For wading, I have a shallower basket without any holes that floats on the surface.

Setting the hook with the rod is generally a bad move in the salt. Hand-over-hand retrieves are great for stripping baskets, but they also have the additional advantage of ensuring that you always strip-strike the fish.

Avoid tangles in your stripping basket by placing the first 2 feet of line (the first strip on your retrieve) outside of the basket before you place the rest of the running line in the basket. This prevents disturbing the line on the bottom of the basket when you pick up the rod and begin casting.

Never bring your head into the basket—if you have to, strip it in outside of the basket.

Get the twists out of your running line while you are changing flies. When changing my fly in the surf or on the jetty, I cut off the fly and cast my line into the current while I am selecting a pattern. The pull of the current on the fly line and leader helps take the twists out. Before tying on the fly, I strip the line in through my pinched fingers to help force any coils out.

To cast effectively in the wind, you can improve your casting, use weighted flies and sinking lines, or position yourself strategically. However, when the wind is in your face, the best thing to do is reel in line and shorten up your casting distances. You are not going to be able to cast as far, so don't kill yourself trying.

New Zealand

John Randolph

Stop fantasizing about the monster fish, pristine water, and breathtaking scenery. Here are some tips to ensure a dream trip to this angling Nirvana.

Ninety percent of the largest trout taken each year in New Zealand are lake fish caught in the fall when they come out of Lake Tongariro (and other lakes) into the tributaries on their spawning runs.

Mouse populations explode about every 7 years, brought on by heavy nut crops in the beech forests, according to guide Andy Trowbridge. At this time, fishing mouse imitations can be deadly for double-digit rainbows and browns that have grown heavy from gorging on the rodents.

Some of the largest stream browns are taken in the Nelson to Hamner Springs region.

Traditionally, the North Island has been called the rainbow island and the South Island the brown island, though both islands have healthy populations of each species. The North Island has more lake fishing for huge trout and more lake-run, prespawn, large-trout fishing than the South Island.

The Te Anau area on the South Island has provided some of New Zealand's newest and best stream sight-fishing. While the area gets heavy rainfall, it is worth consideration.

NEW ZEALAND SEASONS

Season	Months	Water and Weather Conditions
Spring	October–November	rivers are bank full
Late Spring	late November–January	waters warm, rainfall can blow out rivers
Summer	January–March	rivers recede
Late summer	March	hot weather and wind
Autumn	April	low, clear water

Accurate casting (on the first cast) is important. The Achilles heel most Kiwi guides deal with is their client's bad casting. Practice casting into a hat at 30 feet before making the trip.

Learn to cast into the wind. Both the North and South Islands can have brisk winds in the late-summer dry-fly season. To cast a heavily dressed fly into the wind, overline your fast-action rod by one line weight and learn to drive the cast into the wind.

New Zealand's insect biota consists of more terrestrials than aquatic insects, including mayflies. That said, river trout look up and during summer and early fall, and they take well-presented dry flies eagerly. Nothing beats a Royal Wulff on most streams during this period. Keep it simple; improve your casting.

Hire a guide—a good one is worth his weight in gold. They can spot trout where an osprey can't.

If you are elderly, or in bad health, make sure and buy a high quality trip insurance, one that includes medivac. The investment of up to $400 for the insurance is worth the price.

A wading staff should be part of your equipment for New Zealand. Most of your fishing will be wading, and the stream bottoms are bouldery and slippery.

Camo-green lines are required by the guides, and with good reason (the trout are highly line shy). Scientific Anglers makes a good camouflage line.

Techniques and Tactics

nymphing with heavily weighted flies and indicators
dry flies come into play and trout become slightly harder to catch

prime dry-fly season; best time for backpacking and fishing
season's best terrestrial fishing; best time for backpacking and fishing
the most challenging conditions; trout are confined and easier to find; spawning browns

Fishing Etiquette

Paul Weamer

Weather, water releases, hatch activity, and trout receptiveness we cannot change. We can control the way we interact with each other while we are fishing. This important, but often overlooked, code of ethics has a tremendous impact on the quality of any fly-fishing experience.

Boating

Communicate with other fishermen. If you're not sure which side of the river someone is fishing or where to float through a pool packed with boats and waders, then ask the other fishermen how they would like you to proceed around them. Most anglers will appreciate that.

Always float behind wading anglers and other boats. If they are too close to the shore to get behind them, then quietly row to the other side of the river. Try not to row or cast while floating past them.

Get out and walk your boat. Sometimes, especially during low water, it's the only way to move through a pool or riffle without disturbing everyone else's fishing.

Learn to row in the off-season—not the peak of the Green Drake hatch. Some outfitters offer rowing courses with guides as teachers. The guide can take control of the boat during sticky situations. If you want to learn by yourself, practice on a lake or during periods of low fishing pressure.

Give wading anglers plenty of room and the right of way. Never crowd an angler who has walked into a spot. You'll have plenty of opportunities to fish other places when you're drifting. The wader has a limited amount of water. If the river is exceptionally crowded or the fishing is poor, it's okay to ask a wader if you can cast to fish rising beyond their casting range, as long your casting or boat position doesn't interfere with their fishing. Many times they will say yes, but if they do not, move on and find another fish.

Row quietly to the takeout after dark. You might be cold, hungry, and ready for a beer, but that doesn't mean everyone else has stopped fishing. It's difficult to see rising fish after sunset, and the wake and noise from a boat pushing hard to the launch compounds the problem. Judge your time and distance so you can get off of the water without rushing.

Rest Stop

You should always ask the intentions of anglers sitting on the bank or anchored in boats. They may be resting a fish. Do not begin fishing in front of, or near, a wader or another boat just because they aren't casting.

Release your anchor quietly. Hold the rope and ease it into the water. The splash from an anchor dropped into the water will scare your fish and any one else's near you.

Always be respectful on the water. Don't yell or curse loudly. Don't announce how many fish you caught and then ask a guide with clients how many they caught. A guide might be having a tough day and neither the guide nor his/her clients will appreciate your bragging.

Apologize and move on if you screw up—sooner or later everyone does. Try to learn from your mistakes.

Wading

If you're not sure where an upriver boat is headed, then politely reveal where you are fishing and ask the rower to go behind you, if possible. Let your intentions be known—no one can read your mind.

Pick one side of the river to fish and do not switch sides when a boat approaches. Too many times wading anglers cast to one side of the river and quickly cast the other direction, after it's too late for an upriver boat to correct its course. Boats are maneuverable, but changing direction quickly in moving water can be difficult and sometimes impossible.

Stop casting when a boat is behind you. Sometimes it's necessary for a boat to float very close to you to avoid spooking your fish. I've seen careless waders unintentionally hook boaters on their backcast by not paying attention.

continued on page 196

Fishing Etiquette continued

Wade quietly. You'll catch more fish and will not disturb those fishing around you.

Cross the river well above or below another angler whenever possible.

Never stand directly across the river from another angler unless you are fishing a large, deep pool. He may be easing his way out to your fish or may be able to cast farther than you can. Stand across from an angler fishing a big pool only if he cannot reach the fish you are casting to. If you're not sure he can reach the fish, ask.

Never trespass across private property no matter how good the fishing is on the other side.

Breathing Room

Solitude is priceless, and it's a great gift to give yourself or another fisherman whenever possible. If you're lucky enough to be fishing the river on a day with few other anglers, give at least half a pool to another fisherman.

Whether wading or floating, don't "relieve" yourself within plain sight of houses or buildings. You wouldn't like someone doing that in your yard.

Parking Area and Boat Launches

Don't park in boat turn-around areas, even though they are often closer to the river than the parking areas. Several times, I have seen anglers unable to launch their boat due to a parked car in the turn-around. Occasionally, I have watched drift-boat owners almost hit a parked car in these areas while trying to launch their boats.

Do not block the boat-launch areas. Often anglers drive their cars onto the ramp at a boat launch, just to get a look at the river. I have done this myself, occasionally, but only at appropriate times. It's not appropriate to park on a boat launch ramp during the river's busy season. Don't drive onto a boat launch at this time of year unless you're planning to launch a boat.

Boating anglers may retrieve their vehicles, and load their boats, in the order they arrived at the boat launch. It's common, at the most popular launches during the peak season, for a line of anglers to be anchored at a launch, waiting for their turn to remove their boats from the river. Everyone's in a hurry and wants to get home, to eat, to get dry, to do a lot of things. But you must remain patient. I have witnessed near fistfights between anglers who ran to get their car, out of turn, and those still waiting at the launch.

When it is your turn to remove your boat at the launch, get your car, get your boat, and get out. Don't have a talk with your friends, break down your rods, pack your gear, or have a cigarette. You can do all these things after you're off the launch. Guides have to get home, shower, eat, make lunches, and check their gear and boats for the next day's trip—all before they can go to sleep. Other anglers may not be guides, but they may have to work the next day, or maybe they need to get home to be with their families. You may be on vacation—just don't spend it on top of the boat ramp.

Don't shine your headlights toward the river from the boat launch. You will ruin the night vision of any anglers still fishing and blind those trying to navigate to the launch.

Finding Great Lakes Solitude

Rick Kustich

When fish are in, the challenge is not in catching them, it's finding some elbow room. Here's how to beat the crowds.

Prime time is late October and November, and again in March and April. Fish during the "off months." Steelhead, browns, and salmon run as early as August on some streams, and you can have good fishing in midwinter as long as the rivers are free of ice.

Look for cool weather and rain storms that raise stream levels and bring fish in early (September and early October) and late (April and May) in the season. In winter (December–February), days when the air temperatures are above freezing are best.

Fish in foul weather during prime time. If it's cold or raining, there will be less people on the stream. Avoid sunny days.

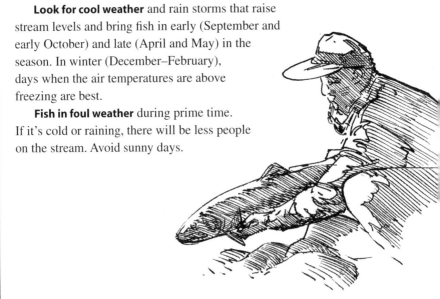

If water rises fast and there's a lot of debris in it, such as leaves, then the fishing shuts down. But once water stabilizes and starts to drop, you can often hook fish in murky water by targeting their holding lies.

Fish late in the day. Most Great Lakes anglers get on the water at the crack of dawn, and the catch-and-keep anglers leave the stream after they fill their limits. Steelhead become active again in the low light of evening.

Dropping and Clearing

Fish when water clarity is dropping and clearing during prime time. That might mean hopping over to a stream that was turbid the day before on the off chance that you can be one of the first there when it starts to clear and the fish go on the grab.

The farther you walk, the better able you are to get away from crowds. You can also float larger streams for solitude.

Fish overlooked water. Most anglers concentrate on the pools, but you can catch fish in small slots and pocketwater and by swinging flies through tailouts.

Fish rivers that typically receive lower annual runs than surrounding rivers. Anglers tend to gravitate to the greatest opportunity to catch fish. Rivers that are not stocked at all and depend on strays from other rivers or on natural reproduction will generally experience lower runs. This is also true of rivers that receive lower plantings than surrounding rivers.

Fish big water. Many anglers are intimidated by bigger sections of river. With two-handed rods and Spey techniques, all water in the Great Lakes region can effectively be covered.

Steelhead

Lani Waller

Be there when they are. Get reliable information anywhere you can. If you drive along a river, you can always tell if the fish are there by the number of vehicles parked by the side of the road.

Most steelhead prefer flies that are moving fairly slowly—about half the current speed. You can fish a steelhead fly too fast, but it is hard to fish it too slowly.

Half the summer-run steelhead that rise to your dry fly should actually take it. If significantly fewer than that take your fly, it means your dry fly is too large.

Pink is a great color for a steelhead fly. In dirty water, hot pink reflects any light penetrating the surface.

Steelhead wet fly

Steelhead prefer to lie close to shore if the current is right, if the water is at least 3 feet deep, and if they have not been disturbed by wading anglers. Fish that water first before wading out to your armpits.

Use fly lines with interchangeable tips to modify the depth you are fishing. Not all runs are created equal.

In the end, a deep fly produces the most strikes.

In clear water, take larger, or more, steps between casts. Slow down when water visibility gets around 2 feet.

Search for fish you cannot see with larger flies that push more water, making it easier for the maximum numbers of fish to see the fly, under the widest range of water depths, surface textures, clarity, and from the greatest distances.

Close the deal on a fish that has risen to a searching pattern but refused it with a smaller fly that pushes less water and makes a smaller surface disturbance. Judge the fly by the size of the surface disturbance it makes on the water, and not the size of the fly. The actual volume of the fly's body is usually only relevant in places where it can be clearly seen by a temperamental or "fussy" fish.

Fast Walk

Most steelhead prefer water speeds about the same as a fast walk. Avoid fast rapids and riffles and slow or stagnant water.

The greater the difference between the fly a fish just refused and the next one you show it, the more likely it will take it. So, if the fish rises to a greased #6 Muddler, and you want to short-circuit the process, don't choose a #8 Muddler as your next fly. Immediately go to a wet fly.

There are no accidents in nature, and no mistakes—only patterns of cause and effect. Everything happens for a reason, and the more of those reasons and connections you know, the clearer your understanding of the patterns of nature become. So remember everything you see when you hook a steelhead—the depth, color, and speed of the water; the light and water temperature.

Steelhead dry flies

How to Catch Trophy Smallmouth Bass

Bob Clouser

To catch large bass consistently requires special techniques.

Improve your casting. You need to be able to make long, accurate casts—often with heavy flies. Learn to make only one (or two, at most) backcasts to present the fly. Lines with heavy front tapers help you cast large flies great distances with minimal false casts.

Fish in big-bass water and focus on big-bass habitat. Big bass prefer areas with deep water, moving currents, and structure with large rocks, sunken trees, large logs, or some other debris that provides a place to escape to—and a hiding place from which to ambush food.

Find unpressured water—whether that means being the first on the water or floating or walking to water that doesn't get hit hard.

Fish early or fish late. At these hours, there are fewer anglers on the water to spook the fish, and large bass are often feeding—sometimes in shallow water.

Hunt heads and cast only to the largest fish. Don't spend time on the splashy risers, look for swells or swirls, or better yet, rolling fish. Small dimples can sometimes mean large fish, and it pays to watch a rising fish to try and determine size. If fishing in clear water where you can spot the fish, don't waste time casting to smaller bass—even though this may be fun, you may not be prepared for a big one when you see it.

Be patient. To catch big bass, wait for them. Smaller bass generally

Give Them the Groceries

Big bass eat big flies. Small flies are fine for small fish, but lure the lunkers with large patterns.

begin rising first, and if you start casting to them, the bigger bass may spook and never rise. Stake out an area and wait—like a hunter waits for his prey.

Be stealthy. Avoid bright clothing and reflective tackle. Pull or drop anchor quietly. Wade slowly so that you don't create a lot of disturbance on the water.

Have good timing. Spring, when bass are spawning, and fall, when bass feed heavily to prepare for winter, are the best times to consistently catch trophies. I prefer not to fish for spawning bass and focus my efforts on fall fishing.

Pay attention to water temperature. Even though spring and fall are prime times, when the water temperatures rise above 85 degrees, big bass need to feed constantly because their metabolisms are at the highest point. On many rivers, you will see them chasing baitfish during a hot summer day.

Fish the rise. Not hatches, rising water. When the water rises as a result of rain or other factors, big bass go on the prowl for the abundance of food that becomes available as water disturbs the bottom debris and knocks insects and crayfish loose from their crevices. High water pushes baitfish out of the heavy current in the center of a river toward the margins along the shore. When baitfish concentrate in these areas, bass move in to feed on them.

Look for mudding carp. Carp feed and disturb the stream bottom and bass often follow behind them, eating crayfish and insects that are kicked up. This is one of the best ways I know to consistently catch large bass in the heat of summer.

Stay sharp. Be prepared to catch the big ones. Take care of your body like you take care of your gear. Stay sharp mentally by drinking enough water and eating nutritious snacks; dress for a wide range of weather conditions. Maintain and care for your gear throughout the year, and check to make sure your hook points are sharp and your tippets aren't frayed or nicked throughout the day. Fish with tackle appropriate for large fish. Always ask yourself, what am I going to do if I hook a monster? Is my tackle up for the job?

Stillwater Carp

Brad Befus

Besides lakes and reservoirs, many golf course, park, and farm ponds contain carp (most likely grass carp) because they help control weed growth.

Target carp feeding in the shallows. Though carp will feed in deeper water, shallow-water fishing is not only exciting but easier to present your fly to a fish that is actively feeding.

In the spring, dark-bottomed bays heat faster, attracting carp.

Klooping fish feed on the surface with an audible popping or sucking noise. They may be eating anything from cottonwood seeds, berries, terrestrials, or aquatic insects. Lead surface feeders so they intercept your fly.

Carp chasing crayfish

Tailing fish are active feeders, rooting along the bottom like redfish, and are only interested in what is right in front of them. You must place your fly within 6 to 8 inches of the fish's window of sight.

Hellraisers are most often spawning fish, identified by their splashes and wallows. These fish are hard to catch and you should focus your efforts on active feeders.

Cruisers—carp swimming along at mid-depth—fall into two categories: spooked and roaming fish. Spooked fish are swimming fast and erratically and aren't worth your efforts. Roaming fish (singles or packs) are worth watching because one or more of them may start to feed.

A slight twitch of any pattern sometimes provokes a strike.

Pick individual targets rather than casting into the middle of large packs of carp. It sometimes pays to watch the fish before casting in case they start to feed.

Walk slowly and try not to push too much water when wading. If in a boat, use a push pole, not a motor.

Strip-strike to give the carp another chance to take the fly if it misses it the first time.

Cast to Feeding Fish

Spend your time casting to feeding carp, not cruising, sunbathing, or spooked fish. Feeding carp are most often either klooping (feeding on the surface) or rooting on the bottom, with their tails tipped and heads down.

West Coast Stripers

Dan Blanton

Advice from an expert guide on the West Coast's finest fishery and good general tips for all saltwater fishing. Visit danblanton.com for more information on this and a wide range of topics.

Hire a guide for one or two outings to help shorten the learning curve if you have never fished San Francisco Bay or the Delta. Some hire two or three different guides to learn more than one approach to the fisheries.

You can cover more water from a boat since shore fishing is limited on the Bay and Delta.

Get good charts learn a section of water at a time. Very important, too, is a good fish finder/depth sounder to locate structure, holes, drop-offs, weed lines, and, of course, bait and fish.

The best tides for fishing the Bay system are the "Neap" tides, which occur on a quarter moon phase. The reason is that the flats where you'll have the greatest chances of success will remain flooded during prime morning time since there will be less exchange of water from high to low tide. Avoid big tidal swings that occur on "Spring" tides.

Delta tides are not as critical, but you do want moving water with the major tide occurring during the daylight hours. On full-moon periods you can still catch fish during the day, but the major tidal flow will be at night and the bass feed most heavily at that time. Fishing at night on the Bay is illegal, but night fishing is permitted on the Delta.

Use 8- to 9-weight rods since you'll be casting fairly large

Blanton's Whistler

and heavy flies. Reels should have a good drag and hold at least 150 yards of backing.

Fast-sinking shooting heads or integrated heads are the most useful lines. You'll also want a slow-sinker for shallower waters, such as a type II or III shooting head. A floating shooting head with an intermediate shooting line is a great choice for tossing poppers, Crease Flies, and Gurglers—upline by at least two weights when using shooting heads. Put 50-pound braided loops on all the lines for attaching leaders and backing. A stripping basket or tub (vertical line management device) helps. I like to use 8 feet of 20-pound Berkley Big Game looped to the braided loop using a surgeon's loop or a Bimini twist loop for a leader with sinking lines. I attach the fly with a Kreh nonslip loop knot.

Top flies: Blanton's Jig Hook Flashtail Whistler; Blanton's Jig Hook Flashtail Clouser; Sar-Mul-Mac; Half & Half; Lefty's Deceiver; Ron Dong Crease Fly; Blados Crease Fly; and Gurglers. Top sizes and colors: 2/0 and 3/0 in white/chartreuse; white/pink/purple; white/brown; white/gray; and black. Bulky flies that push water and sink fast are more productive in turbid waters.

The best retrieves are a mix of full- and half-arm extensions, with several pauses during the retrieve (also called the stop-and-drop technique) to allow the fly to sink like an injured baitfish. Make the fly jump to push some water and attract attention. Short, twitchy, Woolly Bugger retrieves don't work well. Stopping and dropping is particularly important in the Delta once the water temperature falls under 50 degrees.

The right retrieve is often more important than the fly. Always retrieve the fly until the leader hits the rod tip. Hover it on the surface a moment before lifting it for a recast. It's amazing how many fish hit at the last second just as you're lifting the fly.

The best months to fish the Bay are March and April and again in September through November. Midsummer isn't as productive since most of the fish are in the ocean. The best fishing in the Delta begins in September, with October, November, and December producing best; and again in March. If I only had two months to fish the Delta, it would be October and November.

Shad

Brian Wiprud

Shad have quietly been providing anglers from California to Connecticut with amazing fly-rod sport.

Location is everything. Typically tails of rapids are the most likely places to find large numbers of shad. They gather in the pools overnight and ascend the rapids in daylight.

Rising water temperatures between 55 and 72 degrees are ideal; conversely, cooling water works in your favor any time the river reaches 73 degrees, the temperature at which shad spawn and are less inclined to feed. A cool rain or colder tributary that lowers the river tributary can turn distracted spawning fish back to schooling fish ready to strike.

Shad continue to move upriver in bright sun and in the middle of the day. I've often read or heard that shad prefer to move in low light, but my best days are sunny, cloudless days between 10 A.M. and 2 P.M. Early mornings are often productive, but shad drop into deeper water in the pool as the sun rises. When they become accustomed to the brighter conditions (around 10 A.M.), they once again start to move up river into the shallow water of the rapids.

When fishing water 5 feet deep or less, a floating line and a standard downstream swing is the best presentation.

Weight is the most important attribute of a shad fly. It must be heavy enough to reach the fish. If shad are moving toward your fly, but not hitting, add more weight.

Fly color is often debated, but you can't go wrong with pink, red, orange, or chartreuse.

Look for Seams

Shad schools in the ocean often corral prey along current seams and at thermal boundaries. Locations such as strong current seams and tributary confluences that mimic these conditions in rivers can collect large numbers of fish and cause them to feed opportunis-

Precise imitations are less effective than simple patterns that accentuate the basic visual qualities of small crustaceans, primarily their translucent, almost-clear bodies and a small dab of color (either green or pink) in their upper carapace.

Tie or buy flies that ride hook point up to increase the number of hookups in the roof of the mouth (shad's lips are thin and tear easily) and keep the hook point from dulling on the river bottom.

Index